MANAGING YOUR

PERSONAL TAXES

Copyright © Templar Publishing Ltd 1988

First published in Great Britain in 1988
by Ward Lock Limited, 8 Clifford Street, London W1X 1RB
An Egmont Company

Designed and produced by Templar Publishing Ltd
107 High Street, Dorking, Surrey RH4 1QA
Typeset by Servis Filmsetting Ltd, Manchester
Printed and bound in Great Britain
by Richard Clay Ltd
Chichester, Sussex

British Library Cataloguing in Publication Data

O'Brien M.J.
Managing your personal taxes. –
(You and your money series).
    1. Income tax – Great Britain
I Series
336.24'0941   HJ4707

ISBN 0-7063-6670-0

MANAGING YOUR

PERSONAL TAXES

DR. M.J. O'BRIEN

Ward Lock · London

CONTENTS

· 1 ·
THE TAX RETURN

'The Inland Revenue are empowered by the Taxes Management Act to require that any person may be sent a notice by the Inland Revenue and must then deliver back to the Inland Revenue within the time limit on the notice a return of their income computed in accordance with the Income Taxes Acts and specifying each separate source of income and the amount from each source.' These words are a foundation of all tax returns sent out each year and there are some 3.3 million returns sent to those who are self-employed and some 7 million to those who are employed. Tax returns can differ depending upon the individual at whom they are aimed. The most common types are –

● Form P1: This is in the main for people who have relatively straightforward tax affairs.

● Form 11P: This is for employed people with more complicated tax affairs, who usually have to pay the higher rates of tax.

● Form 11: This is for the self-employed.

Examples of these forms for the years 1988/89, that is, for the return of income up to 5th April 1988, are shown as an Appendix to this chapter.

WHO MUST COMPLETE A TAX RETURN?

Anyone who is served with a tax return must complete it and return it to the Inland Revenue, even if they do not believe they are liable to income tax. The tax return serves two purposes: it is both a return of income for a year and a claim for allowances for the following year. The 1988/89 returns shown in this chapter therefore cover the return of income and capital gains for the year ended 5th April 1988, and also claim the allowances that that person is entitled to for the year ended 5th April 1989.

If a tax return has not been sent there is no obligation to fill one in. However, those who are liable to tax, either on income or capital gains, must notify the Revenue that they are so liable no later than one year after the 5th April of that tax year. If someone made a capital gain in the year to 5th April 1986 he would have to

Inland Revenue
Income Tax

Tax return   Income and Capital Gains for year ended 5 April 1988
                Allowances for year ending 5 April 1989

H.M. Inspector of Taxes   Date of issue   Reference   National Insurance no.

Please use the space below if you need to correct your name and address or wish to add any details. Is your postcode correct?

You may avoid delay if you use the reference and National Insurance number shown above when you write to or visit your tax office.

Postcode _____

- You are required to complete this form, sign the declaration on the last page and send it back to me within 30 days.
- Before you start to fill in this form, please read "How to fill in your tax return." Look at each section before you write in your entries.
- If you are a woman and the return is addressed to you, make all your entries in the "Self" boxes and columns.
- If you are a married man and your wife is living with you, you must show all her income and chargeable gains.
- Remember to include all your income, even if you have already paid tax on it.
- Please be brief and give only the details asked for in the notes. If you do need extra space for any section, enter the total on the form and attach a separate piece of paper with the details.
- If you need help or more information, please ask me.

P1(1988)

notify the Revenue he was liable, whether they sent him a return or not, by the 5th April 1987. There are penalties for those who fail to make such a return (see page 153).

TIME LIMITS

The tax returns carry statutory time limits which require the forms to be completed and sent back to the Revenue within thirty days of the date of receipt and each return bears the date of issue. If the return is not sent back within thirty days nothing happens. Indeed the Revenue are normally quite happy so long as people send the returns back within, say, six months of receipt. Delay

Income: 6 April 1987 to 5 April 1988

Trade, profession or vocation

	Business name and address	Type of income	Self	Wife
17-19			£	£
		Enterprise allowance	£	£
20		Balancing charges	£	£
		Deductions for Capital Allowances	£	£
21	Deduction for Class 4 National Insurance contributions enter 'X' here			▶ ☐
	If your profits for Class 4 National Insurance contributions purposes are affected by interest paid, certain capital allowances or losses not given in the assessment, give details on a separate sheet and enter 'X' here			▶ ☐

beyond the six month period is likely to cause problems as the Revenue might not have time to issue a tax assessment before the payment becomes due.

An important part of each tax return is the declaration which comes at the end of the return. This declaration carries the very serious note that '*False statements can result in prosecution.*'

If someone makes an incorrect tax return declaration then the Revenue ultimately reserve the right to prosecute. Whilst this warning is on every one of the 10 to 11 million returns issued each year the actual number of prosecutions in any one year for

**Inland Revenue
Tax Return 1988-89**

Income, Class 4 National Insurance contributions
and Capital Gains for year ended 5 April 1989
Allowances for year ending 5 April 1989

H.M. Inspector of Taxes	Date of issue	Reference	National Insurance no.

You are required to complete pages 2-8 of this form, sign the Declaration on page 8 and send it back to me within 30 days.
It will help if you will also give the information requested below.

*Please read the introduction to the enclosed notes before you start to fill in the form; the notes are there to help you.
Please ask me if you need any further help or information. If you find that there is insufficient room in any section, please attach a separate sheet.*

Pensions information these details will help me to give you the right PAYE code

If you or your wife receive a pension, please give the following details —

Type of pension	Say if it is paid weekly, 4 weekly, monthly or quarterly ➤	Amount(s) you receive Self	Wife

If you or your wife are likely to start receiving a pension before 6 April 1989, please give the following details —

Starting date	Type of pension	Say if it is payable weekly, 4 weekly, monthly or quarterly ➤	Amount(s) you will receive Self	Wife

If you or your wife were born before 6 April 1929, please give date(s) of birth: ➤ Self [ ] Wife [ ]

11P (1988)

---

tax offences is only some 20 to 30, and those prosecuted are
usually people in business who have sent in incorrect accounts.
Nevertheless it is a serious declaration, and no one should sign a
tax return unless they are sure it is correct. They are not
guaranteeing that the return is 100 per cent accurate, merely that
it is correct *to the best of their knowledge and belief.* This can be
an important distinction if the return has been filled in relying on
incorrect information supplied, for example, by a bank. In such
circumstances the taxpayer himself would not be regarded as
guilty of any offence.

A relatively recent development is that tax returns sent to employed people now carry their national insurance number. The Revenue have recently completed their computerisation programme under which all those in employment now have their files held on computer and listed under national insurance numbers. This gives the Revenue easy access to information on each taxpayer's file. For security and confidential reasons the files are held in groups so that it is not possible for a tax officer working in one district to access a file other than those for which he is responsible. This use of technology should, in the future, greatly improve the administration of tax return issues and processing.

WHERE TO FIND HELP

One of the best sources of help which is often overlooked is the comprehensive notes which the Revenue send out with the tax return headed *The Tax Return Guide*. This is intended to help taxpayers fill in the form and though it has no statutory force it does, if read in conjunction with each part of the tax return, provide help in all but the most complex situations. It is also possible to go to the district tax office to discuss any difficulties you may have in making a tax return. If the tax office is difficult to reach, then you can go to the local PAYE Enquiry Office. The addresses can be found in the 'phone book under Inland Revenue.

For those with more complicated affairs it is best to seek the professional advice of either members of one of the accountancy bodies or the Institute of Taxation. The Yellow Pages should provide a good summary of those available in the area listed under 'Accountants'. It must be remembered, however, that there is no legal bar to anyone setting up and calling himself an accountant whereas it is only those who are members of an accountancy body who may use the title Chartered or Certified Accountant. Whilst there are many good non-qualified accountants it is also true to say that there are many poor ones. Unless you can rely on a personal recommendation it is wisest to stick to those who are members of the recognised bodies.

The chapters which follow go through the tax return in the

order of the 11P form, that is, the one for employed people. The box numbers shown are, however, common to most tax returns and so the notes can be easily cross-referenced.

TAX SCHEDULES
While one Income Tax only covers an individual's liability to tax in the United Kingdom, confusion sometimes arises because it is broken down into different Schedules. These are not different taxes, they are simply the means of calculating the income from different sources which is liable to Income Tax. The summary of the Schedules and the type of income which their rules cover are listed below.

Schedule A – This concerns income from property or land.

Schedule B – This covers income from the letting of commercial woodlands. Under the 1988 Finance Bill Schedule B was abolished from 6th April 1988.

Schedule C – This concerns income arising from public revenue dividends payable in the United Kingdom. Basic rate tax would be deducted at source.

Schedule D – This is a complicated Schedule in that it is broken down into six sources of income. The cases are as follows:
Case I: Tax is charged in respect of any trade carried on in the United Kingdom.
Case II: This charges tax in respect of any profession or vocation carried on in the United Kingdom.
Case III: Tax is payable on any interest of money or annuities or annual payments, or discounts and income except that charged under Schedule C from securities bearing interest from Government funds.
Case IV: This charges tax on income arising from securities outside the United Kingdom where such income is not chargeable under Schedule C.
Case V: Tax is chargeable on income arising from possessions outside the United Kingdom, e.g. from an overseas trade or

overseas rental income.

Case VI: This is the sweeping-up section and charges tax on any annual profits or gains not falling under any case of Schedule D and not chargeable under Schedules A, B, C or E.

The rules for Case I and Case II of Schedule D are exactly the same and the rules for Case IV and Case V of Schedule D are themselves not differentiated. The rules for Case III and Case VI are quite separate.

Schedule E – This is the Schedule under which all employment income is taxed. It is divided into three cases.

Case I: Case I of Schedule E charges to tax income from the holding of an office or employment for a person who is currently resident and is ordinarily resident in the United Kingdom.

Case II: Charges tax for a person who is not resident or who is not ordinarily resident in the United Kingdom against any emoluments or rewards for the chargeable period arising from duties performed in the United Kingdom.

Case III: When a person is resident in the United Kingdom, whether ordinarily resident there or not, any emoluments received in the UK in the chargeable period can be taxed under Case III.

Schedule F – Charged under this Schedule is the income from all dividends and other distributions from United Kingdom resident companies. Again, like Schedule C, Income Tax will have been deducted at source from the dividends paid by a company.

· 2 ·
EMPLOYMENT

The United Kingdom tax system incorporates graduated rates of tax so that the more you earn the higher the amount taken away in tax. For most people it is the basic rate of tax which is of most importance and for 1987/88 this is 27 per cent. As the table below shows, income earned in 1987/88 is taxed at 27 per cent on the first £17,900 earned over and above any allowances due. This means that a single person having no other allowances may earn £17,900 plus their personal allowance of £2,425, a grand total of £20,325 before moving into the next tax band rate of 40 per cent. When his income went above £22,825 he would move into the 45 per cent tax bracket, and so on.

The 1988 Finance Bill has radically altered the United Kingdom tax structure both in the number of bands and also the fact that the maximum rate of tax has been brought down from 60 to 40 per cent. For most people the most important change will have been the reduction in basic rate to 25 per cent, which applies to the first £19,300 of taxable income.

TABLE 1 – Rates of Tax

		1986–87 Bands £29%	1987–88 Bands £27%	1988–89 Bands £25%
Basic Rate		1–17,200	1–17,900	1–19,300
Higher Rates	40%	17,201–20,200	17,901–20,400	Over 19,300
	45%	20,201–25,400	20,401–25,400	–
	50%	25,401–33,300	25,401–33,300	–
	55%	33,301–41,200	33,301–41,200	–
	60%	Over 41,200	Over 41,200	–

The taxable income shown in the above table is after taking all other allowances into account – mortgage interest relief, personal allowances, business expansion scheme relief, industrial buildings allowances, and so on. Tax is levied on the net amount. In the 1987/88 tax year you would have to earn at least £43,000 per year to have any of your income taxed at 60 per cent. Only 5 per cent of taxpayers are taxed at the higher rates and this is true for all the years shown in the tables. Despite this, the higher-rate taxpayers provide a large percentage of the actual net income taken by the Revenue. In 1987/88 the figure is estimated to be 29 per cent with a reduction to 27 per cent following the drastic changes to the UK tax structure in 1988/89.

See note	Income: 6 April 1987 to 5 April 1988		
1-3	**Employment, etc.**		
	Earnings (including fees, bonus, commission, etc) from duties performed wholly in the UK	Self	Wife
	Occupation and employers name(s) and address(es)	£	£

Box 1–3 OWN EARNINGS

At the end of each year the employer should provide a form P60 giving full details of all the amounts earned in the year together with the amount of tax which has been deducted. The details from this form should be included on the tax return, showing one amount for self and separate details for a wife if she is also in employment. If there is more than one employer there will be a P60 form for each employment and more than one set of figures will have to be included.

If the figures are not readily available the tax return should still show the type of work and the employer's name and address but you may write for both wife and self 'per PAYE' if it is known that the amounts involved were subjected to the PAYE tax deduction scheme. For many people the entries in box 1 to 3 of the tax return would be the only entry that they make, and even that will be 'per PAYE'. You can leave the balance of the return blank if none of the other boxes are relevant.

WIFE'S EARNINGS ELECTION

In the UK system of taxation until April 1990 a wife's income is added to her husband's and taxed as if it is his, subject to the fact that any allowances to which she is entitled will be set against the total income. Suppose, for example, both husband and wife earned £20,000 per year in 1987/88. If they were single, each of them would be liable only to the basic rate of tax. By getting married they fall into a tax trap: all £40,000 is now taxed on the husband. Against this he can set his own married man's allowance and his wife's earned income allowance, but the total will still leave them liable to the higher rate of tax, since the net amount of £33,780 would be over the threshold for 55 per cent tax.

The Inland Revenue recognise this disadvantage by allowing both husband and wife an option under which they can choose, or elect, for separate taxation of the wife's earned income as if she was a single person. This does not, however, apply to any investment income she might have, which will be assessed on the husband in the normal way except that he receives the single personal allowance instead of the married man's allowance. Though the wife's earnings continue to be shown on the husband's tax return they are taxed separately. Any election must be made in writing, and in this case it has to be submitted on a special form which the Revenue will supply.

An election for 1986/87 may be worthwhile if the joint total incomes of the husband and wife, before deduction of personal allowances and reliefs, is at least £26,521, but will not generally be worthwhile for incomes lower than this. The wife's share of this £26,521, if it was her income which was the lower, would have to be at least £6,986. If the combined income is higher the minimum income of the less well-off partner reduces, but it must never become lower than £4,890. For 1987/88 an election will not be beneficial unless the combined incomes are at least £26,870 with the lower income at that point being at least £6,545.

For 1988/89 an election will normally be worthwhile only if the couple's combined income before deduction of allowances and reliefs is at least £28,484, including a wife's earned income of at least £6,579. The Inland Revenue leaflet IR13 which can be obtained from tax offices gives further details of the election to be made.

The reason for the variation in the level of the less well-off

Example 1

Husband earns £20,000
Wife earns £8,000

The allowances for 1987/88 are:
Married man's allowance £3,795, wife's earned income allowance and single person's allowance £2,425.

Without Election

Total earnings	£28,000
less married man's allowance	3,795
less wife's earned income allowance	2,425
Total taxable income	£21,780

Tax due

Tax @ 27% on £17,900	£4,833
Tax @ 40% on £2,500	1,000
Tax @ 45% on £1,380	621
TOTAL	£6,454

With Election

Husband's earnings	£20,000	Wife's earnings	£8,000
less personal allowance	2,425	less personal allowance	2,425
Total taxable income	£17,575	Total taxable income	£5,575

Total tax @ 27%:   Husband £4,745.25   Wife £1,505.25

TOTAL   £6,250.50

partner's income as the other partner's income rises is that an election for the wife's earnings to be taxed separately means that the husband loses his married man's allowance. In the 1987/88 tax year this difference means that £1,370 of allowances will be lost and therefore taxed at at least 40 per cent, that is at a cost of £548. It is thus only when a relatively large amount of the wife's income is being charged at higher-rate tax that the earnings election becomes beneficial.

The calculation to do is set out opposite.

In this particular case a saving might be expected from the use of the election, and as the example shows the saving is £203.50. The more the couple earns the greater the tax saving can be.

It must be stressed that these figures are for guidance only. The inclusion of any additional allowances can have a substantial

---

Example 2

Without election

Total taxable income as before	£21,780
less Building Society interest	2,000
	£19,780
Tax due on £17,900 @ 27%	£4,833
Tax due on £1,880 @ 40%	752
Total tax due	£5,585

With election

Husband's total taxable income as before	£17,575
less Building Society interest	2,000
Taxable earnings	£15,575
Tax @ 27%	£4,205.25
Wife's tax as before	1,505.25
Total tax due	£5,710.50

---

effect on the calculation. If, for instance, in Example 1 the couple had also paid £2,000 worth of building society interest during the year on a mortgage the figures would have been quite different.

To make the election in these circumstances therefore costs some £125.50 extra tax. The reason is that in Example 2 when the wife's income is added to the husband's, bringing him into the higher tax bracket, the building society interest is relieved at either 40 or 45 per cent tax, whereas with an election it is only relieved at 27 per cent.

SEPARATE ASSESSMENT

This is not to be confused with wife's earnings election which can save tax, or sometimes lose it if the election is incorrectly made. The option for separate assessment makes no difference to a couple's total tax bill. What it does mean is that the bill is split differently so that each partner becomes legally responsible for their share.

MAKING THE ELECTIONS

A wife's earnings election for the year 1987/88 should be made jointly before 6th April 1989, and must be on Form 14 which will be supplied by the Revenue. It remains in force until both husband and wife ask for it to be withdrawn. A decision to withdraw an election must be made before the 6th April following the year to which it is to relate, so that an election for 1987/88 would have to be withdrawn by 6th April 1989.

An election by either spouse for separate assessment is made to the Revenue on Form 11S and must be made before 6th July in the year to which it relates so that an election to opt for separate assessment of Income Tax for 1987/88 must be made before 6th July 1987. It remains in force until withdrawn by whoever made the original application. A separate application is required for Capital Gains Tax.

INDEPENDENT TAXATION

The Treasury issued a Press Release on 15th March 1988 announcing that from April 1990 husbands and wives will be taxed independently. The intention is to provide independent taxation for husbands and wives and to give complete privacy for married women so that they are no longer considered merely to be their husband's chattel for tax purposes. It is also wished to

---

Example

Present system		**New System:**	
		Independent Taxation	
Husband	£	*Husband*	£
Own earnings	10,000	Earnings	10,000
Wife's earnings	2,000	Less personal	
Wife's investment		allowance	2,605
income	500	Less married	
Total income	12,500	couple's	
less married man's		allowance	1,490
allowance	4,095	so pays tax at 25%	
		on	5,905
less wife's earned		so tax bill is	1,476.25
income			
allowance	2,000*		
so pays tax at 25%			
on	6,405		
so tax bill is	1,601.25		
Wife		*Wife*	
Wife's income taxed		Earnings	2,000
as husband's		Investment income	500
		less personal	
		allowance	2,605
		so tax bill is	0

Rest of allowance cannot be used.

end the tax penalties that currently arise when a couple who have been living together get married.

From 1990 no wife's earnings election will be necessary because her earnings and investment income will not be added to her husband's. As now, the majority of taxpayers will not receive tax returns but if one is needed for a married woman's income it will be sent to her direct and she will be required to fill it in. There will therefore be no necessity for married women in future to have to tell their husbands what their earnings or other income are. An example of how the new system will work is set out on page 21, and for the sake of illustration shows tax rates and allowances at 1988/89 levels.

This example shows the tax bill, under the present system and under independent taxation, for a couple where the husband earns £10,000; the wife earns £2,000 from a part-time job and has £500 investment income. Tax rates and allowances are shown at 1988/89 levels.

Under independent taxation, the wife will pay no tax on her income at all, whereas previously her husband had to pay on her £500 investment income.

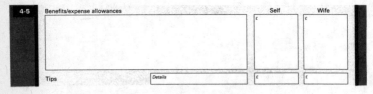

Box 4 – 5 *BENEFITS/EXPENSE ALLOWANCES*

Certain benefits or allowances received in an employment are subject to tax. The rules vary according to whether you are in lower-paid or higher-paid employment, that is, earning more than £8,500 per annum.

Lower paid

If employees receive something which they can turn into cash they are taxable on the second-hand value of what is received. If an employee receives a suit from his employer then he will be taxable on the second-hand value of the suit and not on the cost to the employer. Normally this would be about one third of the full cost. Similarly, if the employer gives Christmas turkeys or bottles of whisky to his staff then the employees are taxable on the second-hand value of the gifts. The second-hand value will, naturally, vary according to the gift, and is always negotiable. Any amounts which are paid by way of a voucher will usually be taxable in full on the cost of the voucher, so if the employee receives a voucher to go and claim his suit then it is the cost of the voucher that matters and not the cost of the suit.

When actual expense allowances are given in cash then that will normally be the amount which should go down as the gross sum. A tax return later on allows for legitimate business expenses to be claimed as a deduction from the expense allowance, and it may well be possible to reduce the amount taxable to nil.

If a benefit is received by the lower paid which cannot be converted to cash then it is not taxable. This could cover items such as the use of a company car, for which no taxable benefit would be incurred if the earnings were under £8,500. Similarly, if the employer paid a taxi firm directly to take its lower-paid employees home late at night, that wouldn't be convertible to cash and so would not be a taxable benefit. It would be quite different if the employer gave the employee the cash to pay the taxi driver. In this case the employee would be taxed on the money he had received.

Lower-paid employees can expect their employer to have made a return of the various benefits which they may enjoy in their employment, and it is usually sufficient therefore to write 'per P9D' in the space provided. If certain benefits are known about it does no harm to list them and then to put amounts 'as returned on P9D.' The difficulty is often that the employee does not see what goes on the P9D so that if the entry is incorrect his tax return would be incorrect. The Revenue would not normally take issue with the employee for this but rather with his employer.

If you are earning more than £708.33 per month you will be considered higher paid, even if you only work for three to four months of a year at that rate. In working out whether you earn £8,500 or not it is important to take into account all the potential benefits which might be taxed. Suppose we rate the benefit of having a company car at £500, then an employee who earns £8,100 and has no other benefit other than the use of a company car would be liable for tax on that car, because his total remuneration including the benefits assessable would be £8,600. If he had earned only £7,900 the benefit of the car would not have been taxable because his total earnings would still have been below the £8,500 ceiling. You therefore have to be very careful in noting all the expense allowances received, since even if they are fully claimable such benefits are added to your earnings when calculating whether or not you are higher paid. Once you fall into the higher paid category then the more generous treatment afforded to the lower paid in the taxation of benefits is lost.

Higher paid

Higher-paid employees are taxable on all the benefits they receive from their employment. If, for example, you were given a suit by your company you would be charged on the full cost of the suit and not on its second-hand value. Returns of benefits for higher-paid employees are done on Form P11D by their employer and therefore it should usually be sufficient to write 'per P11D' against the benefits entry of the tax return. Again in doing this you take the chance that the employer is actually returning the benefits correctly on Form P11D and before writing this entry you would be well advised to examine your own personal P11D to ensure that all the benefits you know of have been correctly returned.

Common benefits

The company car and/or private fuel is probably the most common benefit and the Revenue have introduced a scale of charges to give a rough-and-ready measure of what amount should be added to the remuneration in order to calculate people's tax liabilities for receiving the benefit. The tables for 1986/87, 1987/88, 1988/89 are as follows.

The car benefits rates shown for 1988/89 are much higher than those originally proposed because the 1988 Finance Bill doubled the previous 1987/88 figure rather than simply increasing

Table showing car benefit

Age of car at 5th	1988/9		1987/8		1986/7	
April (years)	Under 4	Over 4	Under 4	Over 4	Under 4	Over 4
Original market value up to £19,250			£19,250		£19,250	
Under 1300cc ..	–	–	–	–	£450	£300
Under 1400cc ..	£1,050	£700	£525	£350	–	–
1301cc to 1800cc	–	–	–	–	£575	£380
1401cc to 2000cc	£1,400	£940	£700	£470	–	–
More than 1800cc	–	–	–	–	£900	£600
More than 2000cc	£2,200	£1,450	£1,100	£725	–	–
Original market value between £19,251–£29,000	£19,251–£29,000		£19,251–£29,000		£19,251–£29,000	
	£2,900	£1,940	£1,450	£970	£1,320	£875
Original market value over ... £29,000	£29,000		£29,000		£29,000	
	£4,600	£3060	£2,300	£1,530	£2,100	£1,400

it by the expected 10 per cent. The reasoning given by the Chancellor was that higher rates of tax had now come down and because it was widely recognised that the present car scale rates substantially undervalued the full benefit of having a company car, those who benefited should pay at a rate much nearer to the value of the vehicle provided. His budget speech also suggested that the substantial increase might be repeated in 1989/90. There was, however, no corresponding substantial increase in the car fuel benefit.

The above table relates to benefits assessable for cars provided for business use but available for private use. Insubstantial business use is defined as less than 2,500 miles per year and the taxable benefit for such cars is charged at $1\frac{1}{2}$ times the normal scale charge figure. If more than 18,000 miles' business use is done in a year the scale charge is reduced to 50 per cent of the table figure.

Car fuel benefit			
	1988/9	1987/8	1986/7
	All cars	All cars	All cars
Under 1300cc . .	–	–	£450
Under 1400cc . .	£480	£480	–
1301cc to 1800cc	–	–	£575
1401cc to 2000cc	£600	£600	–
More than 1800cc	–	–	£900
More than 2000cc	£900	£900	–

A separate charge is made where any private petrol is paid by the employer, even if it is only one pennyworth per year. Like the car benefit charge the amount is reduced by 50 per cent if more than 18,000 miles business mileage is done per year. It should be noted that business travel means travelling when required to do so in the performance of the duties of employment and does *not* include travelling between home and the ordinary place of work.

CAR PARKING
If the employer provides parking facilities for his employees then the Revenue has argued that this in principle is a taxable benefit for the higher-paid employee, and also for the lower-paid employee if the employer reimburses his parking charges. However, in practice it was quite difficult to collect the tax due on the benefit and from 6th April 1988 the Inland Revenue have been authorised not to pursue such liabilities. The exemption applies also to any benefit for previous years where such liabilities had not been agreed by 5th March 1988.

BENEFICIAL LOANS
There is a taxable benefit if the employer provides loans at less than the official rate of interest, which varies regularly but is

currently $10\frac{1}{2}$ per cent as from 6th December 1987. If you receive from your employer a loan carrying an interest rate of less than this amount, the difference in the interest rate that you pay and that charged at $10\frac{1}{2}$ per cent is taxable since it counts as a benefit. The majority of loans of this kind provided by employers relate to property. If the property concerned is one on which you would have been entitled to tax relief had you paid interest at the full rate, then there will be no benefit and therefore no tax due, even if the loan is interest free, so long as the loan still outstanding to the employer totals no more than £30,000. If it is greater than £30,000 then there will be a calculation due of the amount of benefit. This is best illustrated by an example.

Mr X works for a building society and receives a loan of £30,000 at 5 per cent and a further £10,000 from his employer at 12 per cent. In the year in question the beneficial loan interest rate was 12 per cent. The benefit is calculated as follows:
Interest charged at beneficial loan interest rate
£40,000 × 12% = £4,800.
Interest paid £30,000 at 5% = £1,500
          £10,000 at 12% = £1,200
Total: £2,700
Difference: £2,100
Benefit charged $\dfrac{£10,000}{£40,000} \times £2,100 = £525$

Therefore £525 would be added to Mr X's taxable earnings in order to calculate the full amount taxable. If he had borrowed the £10,000 from a different organisation such as his bank at 12 per cent interest there would have been no benefit assessable, but because both loans had come from his employer they are lumped together in calculating whether any benefit has been gained.

EXPENSE ALLOWANCES
In general expense allowances are intended to do no more than reimburse the employee for the cost of doing something for business purposes. If this is the case then no taxable benefit is likely to arise. However, there are many occasions when an

allowance is paid which is taxable and which has not been cleared with the Revenue (see **Dispensations** below). This means that the expense payment received must be added to the employee's earnings. This can be something as simple as a lunch allowance or a higher than allowable mileage rate for private use of an employee's car. The Revenue are currently prepared to accept approximately 29p per mile as being the break-even point above which an employee will benefit from any mileage allowance he receives from his employer. They do not accept that any meal allowance can be paid unless the employee is out of the office on business for over a certain period. The type of allowances paid to civil servants is a guide to what is likely to be acceptable to the Revenue. The day subsistence rates to civil servants at 1st August 1987 were as follows:

More than 5 hours absence from the office = £2.85
More than 10 hours absence from the office = £6.25

If the expense reimbursement is for entertaining a client then the Revenue will normally accept that no benefit arises for the employee. However, it should still be shown as income in the relevant part of the tax return but with the full deduction claimed for the reimbursed expense.

Overnight Allowances

Employees are often required to stay overnight on business, and if they do no more than take their hotel bills and have them repaid by their employer there should normally be no problem. Sometimes, however, to save on administration overnight allowances are paid purely because the employee is away on business and no proof is required that he has incurred the expense. The Revenue will normally agree an allowance for this when granting a dispensation (see below). Rates paid to civil servants for overnight work will give some indication of the amounts which are likely to be acceptable.

These are the rates which will be paid for occasional visits, but if people regularly visit any particular area or spend more than 30 days at any one time working in a particular spot the Revenue would expect these rates to be substantially reduced. The maximum levels which are likely to be allowed for long stays will

Night Subsistence

Normal rates	Class 1	Class 2	Class 3
Inner London	£81.90	£55.75	£46.85
Elsewhere	£66.55	£47.20	£35.75

Lodging allowances

Married Officer	Class 1 and Class 2	Class 3
Inner London	£26.10	£19.55
Elsewhere	£22.75	£17.40

Single Householder	All Classes
Inner London	£18.35
Elsewhere	£15.75

be in accordance with the Revenue's lodging allowance payments. It must be stressed that the above figures are for guidance only and there is no absolute right to make those payments unless they are agreed by the Revenue.

Dispensations
It is in both the employers' and the Revenue's interest to simplify the amount which has to be returned on forms P11D or P9D to those items which would actually yield tax. Accordingly employers may approach the Revenue to obtain what is called a 'dispensation' for certain expenses and fringe benefits paid, such as mileage, meal or overnight allowances. Dispensation will be granted if the Revenue accepts that on a broad treatment comparing all employees no actual benefit is being obtained. This is not to say that on certain occasions some employees will not make money out of the allowances.

If a dispensation is granted it means that there is no need to return the allowance paid on form P11D and no requirement actually to incur the expense so long as you really are away on business and entitled to the relevant expense allowance.

This unique advantage of dispensations can be illustrated by a real-life case concerning a Revenue inspector who regularly had to attend different tax districts some miles away from home. He was entitled to receive the overnight allowance shown above for Class 2 staff. He didn't particularly like staying in hotels, so he towed his caravan around and stayed in that every night. Over each six-week period, totalling some 30 working days, he was able to claim a figure of 30 × £47.20, i.e. some £1,416. This was effectively a tax-free payment to him. If the employer (who in this case was the Inland Revenue and therefore no doubt had influence in the matter) had not succeeded in obtaining a dispensation for the payment the £1,416 would have been entirely taxable.

It must be remembered that you don't necessarily pay tax on the full amount of benefits and expense allowances on your tax return, as you will nearly always be able to make some claim against the amounts received.

TIPS

If in the course of your employment you are accustomed to receiving tips, then the amounts should be entered on the tax return. If the tips are doled out by your employer they should have been subject to Pay As You Earn. In any event they are always taxable and therefore should be declared by all those in the kind of business likely to receive tips, such as bar assistants, waiters, hairdressers, taxi drivers and so on.

6	Leaving payments and compensation	Details		£		£	
				Self		Wife	
7	If you or your wife received a taxed sum from the trustees of an approved profit sharing scheme, enter an "X" here			☐		☐	
	If the sum is included in the income shown above, enter an "X" here			☐		☐	
8	Earnings from duties performed wholly or partly abroad			Self		Wife	
	Employment concerned			£		£	
	Dates absent from UK when working abroad. Enclose statement if necessary.			To claim dedn enter "X"	☐		☐

Box 6 *LEAVING PAYMENTS AND COMPENSATION*

When leaving an employment it is normal to receive an amount in

lieu of holiday pay or money already earned but not yet included in a wage slip. These payments are taxed in the normal way, even if received after the employment itself has terminated. Others, however, are tax free. The items which are tax free include:
● Any lump sum received for an injury or disability which meant that you couldn't carry on a job. This would also include a payment made to a widow because her husband had died while carrying on his employment.
● Compensation for the loss of a job done entirely or substantially outside the United Kingdom.
● Lump-sum payments from the employer's pension scheme.
● Money the employer pays into a retirement annuity benefit scheme.

POTENTIALLY TAXABLE LEAVING PAYMENTS
There is a further category of leaving payments which are tax free provided that added together they total less than £30,000. This limit applies to payment of lump sums on leaving an employment or for any other reason, occurring on or after 6th April 1988. Before that date the tax-free limit was £25,000, but between £25,000 and £50,000 the tax due was reduced by 50 per cent. There was a further slice of relief between £50,000 and £75,000 in that the tax due was reduced by 25%. Anything above £75,000 was taxed as normal income.

The payments which go to make up this class of leaving payment which are added together to see if they exceed the £25,000 (1987/88) or £30,000 (1988/89) limit are:

● Any non-contractual payment in lieu of notice. A payment stipulated in your contract of employment in lieu of notice would be taxable as normal earnings.
● Any redundancy payment made under the government's redundancy payment scheme.
● Any compensation payment made for loss of office or for an ex-gratia purpose which is not paid under the terms and conditions of service or where there was a valid expectation of receiving such a payment as part of the reward for services. It is, therefore, essential that any compensation payment which is to be

within this potentially non-taxable category is not contractual and apparently at least not expected by the employee.

If the employer deducts tax from any of the payments shown above which should be tax-free then a tax rebate can be claimed.

The entry for the tax return should show any amount received with a note saying what it was, for example, an ex-gratia payment.

Certain leaving payments and compensation may end up being fully taxable. This is most often the case when either the payments are made before the employment has formally ended or when the contract drawn up gives the employee contractual rights to compensation on severance. Any other assets received, such as being allowed to keep the company car, are taken into account as part of the total.

GOLDEN HALLOS

Though a relatively new phenomenon, it is not now uncommon for certain people to receive inducements to take up an employment. This is commonly called a 'golden hallo.' Some people have argued that such hand-outs could come within the leaving payment and compensation rules mentioned above, being either completely tax free or subject to the exemption limits. This is not the Revenue's view. Any inducement payments are considered to be fully taxable as part of the earnings from the new employment, even if they are phrased in such a way that they are presented as compensation for leaving the old employment. Any golden hallos should, therefore, be entered in full on the tax return.

Box 7 **PROFIT SHARING**

Many employers have in the past set up employee trust schemes, under which certain sums have been paid into the trust by the company, for which they would have received a tax deduction. The trust then pays out amounts to the employees in a form of profit sharing. It used to be possible for companies to make substantial national insurance savings on the amounts paid to employees using the trust route. This advantage has been withdrawn from October of 1987, except for older trusts.

If a payment has been received then it is simply a matter of putting a cross in the box on the return for either yourself or your wife. The sum will have had Pay As You Earn tax deducted and so may have already been included in the income shown under Box 1 to 4 for employment. If this is the case a second cross should be made indicating that the amount has already been included above. If the trust operates a separate PAYE scheme it will not be included in the details above and the Revenue will obtain details from the trust separately.

Box 8 *EARNINGS FROM DUTIES PERFORMED WHOLLY OR PARTLY ABROAD*

If you are normally resident in the United Kingdom a substantial tax saving can be made from working wholly or partly abroad, provided no more than 62 days are spent in the UK out of a continuous period of 365 days. If you are within the 62-day limit then there is a second calculation to do to see whether tax exemption is due. The calculation is as follows:

A The total number of days spent abroad before the first visit back to the UK.
B The total number of days spent in the UK prior to next going abroad.
C The total number of days spent abroad before next returning to the UK.

If B is more than one-sixth of A plus B plus C, then the continuous period is broken and a new period starts from when the taxpayer next returns abroad. The total continuous period must be at least 365 days in order to obtain any relief but there is no limit to its length. The 365 days can cover two tax years. Suppose, for example, you first went abroad for 30 days and then returned for seven days before leaving again for another 20 days abroad. The calculation would be $\frac{7}{57}$, which is less than one sixth, so the 57 days can be the start of a continuous 365-day period. If you then stay in the UK for five days before going abroad for 100 days the total period becomes $\frac{12}{162}$, which is again less than one sixth. This calculation is repeated until the magic 365-day period is reached.

If you spend this continuous period abroad 100 per cent of your earnings for work done *outside* the UK will not be taxed in the UK. This is not to say, of course, that there will not be any foreign tax to pay.

DOUBLE TAXATION RELIEF

If duties are carried out abroad but the earnings do not qualify for the 100 per cent exemption then they will, for a UK resident, be fully taxable in the United Kingdom. Relief will usually be given for any foreign tax paid so long as this does not exceed the UK tax due. If the foreign tax is higher, relief is given by waiving any further UK tax charges. A note of any foreign tax incurred should always be included on a tax return.

TRAVELLING EXPENSES

Those who work abroad for a UK employer will often have their expenses paid for their own travelling, together with any hotel or other expenses, plus visits for their families including children. As long as the travelling expenses paid are because the employment can only be done abroad and the expenses relating to wife and family are for no more than two trips per person per year, there will be no UK tax to pay on the amounts received.

If the employer did not pay the cost of travel and hotel expenses it would not be possible to claim the expenses incurred as a deduction from the earnings received.

CONCEPTS OF UK RESIDENCE

Someone is always resident in the United Kingdom if he spends at least six months of the year there. He is also treated as resident if, over a period of four years, he spends an average of at least three months per year in the United Kingdom. Other than these general rules the decision often hinges on whether he has accommodation available in the United Kingdom. If he does, then he will be treated as UK resident, even if he only visits the United Kingdom for one day in a tax year and does not actually visit the available accommodation. An individual may be resident in many countries and the double taxation rules exist to exempt him from being taxed in more than one country.

A person may be non-resident in the United Kingdom in a year but may still be 'ordinarily resident' there perhaps because he has gone on a year-long cruise, for example. This is taken to mean those who habitually live in the UK although they may have gone on a long holiday. It is thus possible still to be liable to UK taxation even though you are not resident in the period.

DOMICILE

The third concept to take into account is domicile. Under UK law a person may only have one domicile and that will usually be their domicile of origin, that is where they were born. It is possible to change your domicile by going to live in another country for a number of years and cutting all your ties with your domicile of origin, in which case you can acquire a domicile of choice. But if, say, your domicile of origin was France and you maintained a home there and intended going back when your UK employment ceased or on retirement, then you would retain your French domicile even if you stayed in the United Kingdom for thirty years.

ADVANTAGES OF NON-RESIDENCE OR NON-UK DOMICILE STATUS

If someone is non-UK resident he will only be taxed in the United Kingdom on the amount earned here and not on his world-wide income. A UK resident and ordinarily resident person is taxable on all earnings, wherever they arise. Where the duties of an office or employment are performed wholly outside the United Kingdom and the emoluments are foreign then there is no UK tax. Foreign emoluments are the earnings of a non-UK domiciled person from an office outside the United Kingdom with a company which is not resident in the United Kingdom.

If a non-UK domiciled person had foreign emoluments and brought the money into the United Kingdom then he would be taxed in the UK on this amount. If someone had earned £10,000 in the year and brought only £1,000 into the United Kingdom in that year, then it is only the £1,000 on which he would be taxed. If earnings are brought into the UK for an earlier period when the non-UK domiciled person was resident in the UK, he would be taxed in the year when they were brought in, effectively on a receipts basis.

DAY OF ABSENCE FROM THE UNITED KINGDOM

If someone is absent from the United Kingdom at midnight, working or travelling on business, then that day counts as a day of absence. But if he is present in the United Kingdom at midnight he is not entitled to include it as a day of absence. Therefore if someone works in the United Kingdom until 11.30 p.m. of a particular day and then catches a plane to Paris that counts as a day of UK absence, and if he works in Paris until 10.30 p.m. and then flies back to the UK, arriving at 11.15 p.m., that will count as a day of UK presence. When calculating the B/A + B + C fraction above, therefore, great care must be taken to ensure that spending a few hours extra in the United Kingdom does not break a period of 100 per cent foreign income deduction.

· 3 ·
PENSIONS AND BENEFITS

		Self	Wife
11	**Social Security pensions and Benefits** Retirement or old person's pension. If wife's pension (or part of it) is paid by virtue of her own contributions' enter an "X" here ▶ ☐	£	£
12	Unemployment or Supplementary benefits *enter the full taxable amount*	£	£
13	Widows and other benefits - *say what type (from order book)* ☐	£	£

	Pension from former employer and other pensions	Self	Wife
14-15	Name and address of payer(s)	£	£

Box 11   RETIREMENT OR OLD PERSONS' PENSIONS

The entry to be included here is the total amount received in the year, including any age addition which is only payable to pensioners over 80. A wife who obtains her old age pension by virtue of her own contributions should enter an 'X' in the box, since that would allow her to claim wife's earned income allowance against the amount received. This allowance is due even if the husand has chosen to take a married man's pension with his wife giving up any pension she was entitled to on her own account. When the pension is received weekly or quarterly the amount entered should be based upon the weekly rate of entitlement rather than the quarterly payments actually received. Pensions from former employers are dealt with separately: we are only dealing here with social security pensions.

Box 12   UNEMPLOYMENT OR SUPPLEMENTARY BENEFITS

Subject to the notes below on tax-free items all pensions and social security benefits are in the main taxed as earned income and must be entered. This particularly applies to supplementary benefit or unemployment benefit arising from unemployment. Statements should be supplied to claimants by their benefit offices setting out the amounts they have received which are taxable.

Benefits taxable as earned income under Schedule E are shown in the first list. Benefits not taxable are shown in the second list.

Taxable benefits

Industrial death benefit (if paid as pension)
Invalid care allowance
Invalidity allowance when paid with retirement pension
Job release allowance (earlier than one year before
    pensionable age)
Old person's pension
Retirement pension
Statutory maternity pay
Statutory sick pay
Supplementary benefit or income support when paid to
    unemployed and strikers after 4th July 1982
Unemployment benefit after 4th July 1982
Widowed mother's allowance
Widow's allowance
Widow's pension

Non-taxable benefits

Attendance allowance
Child benefit
Child dependency additions paid with widow's allowance,
    widowed mother's allowance, retirement pension, invalid
    care allowance, unemployment benefit or supplementary
    benefits
Child's special allowance
Christmas bonus for pensioners
Death grant
Employment rehabilitation allowance
Fares to school
Gallantry Awards e.g. VC Pensions/Annuities
Guardian's allowance
Income Support*
Invalidity allowance when paid with invalidity pension
Invalidity pension (contributory or non-contributory)
Job release benefit (within one year of pensionable age)
Job search and employment transfer scheme benefits

Maternity grant
Mobility allowance after 6th April 1982
One parent benefit
Severe disablement allowance
TOPS training allowances and grants under similar
   Government schemes for those undergoing training
War orphan's pension
War widow's pension

Short-term benefits

Maternity allowance
Sickness benefit

War disablement benefits

Disablement pension, including
   Age allowance
   Allowance for lowered standard of occupation
   Clothing allowance
   Comforts allowance
   Constant attendance allowance
   Exceptionally severe disablement allowance
   Severe disablement occupational allowance
   Treatment allowance
   Unemployability allowance

*Income support replaced supplementary benefit and is tax free unless paid to the unemployed, those on short-time work, or strikers.

Amounts received from foreign governments may also be tax free, e.g. annuities and pensions payable under any special provision made by the law of the Federal Republic of Germany or any part of it or Austria for victims of National Socialist persecution. Similarly payments by a foreign government of benefits equivalent to those which are tax free in the UK will not be taxed in the UK.

Box 13   *WIDOW'S AND OTHER BENEFITS*

You should enter any amount received for widow's or widowed mother's allowance, widow's pension, widow's industrial death benefit or invalid care allowance. The entry should show all the amounts received in the tax year. The pension book should be consulted to ensure that the description of the pension received is accurate. The question of allowances for widows is dealt with below.

Box 14   *PENSIONS FROM FORMER EMPLOYER AND OTHER PENSIONS*

A pension from a former employer is always taxed. The gross sum received should be shown on the tax return. The name and address of the payer of the pension should also be given, but if this is the same as in previous years you may simply put 'as last year'. If Pay As You Earn is being operated, as is likely, then an entry can be made 'as per PAYE' rather than searching for the exact amount received in the year.

Box 15

This includes pensions from abroad and you should enter the full amount payable for the year whether or not it was received in the United Kingdom. People not domiciled in the United Kingdom will not be taxed on monies not brought into the United Kingdom and a note should be made to this effect. Also there are certain double taxation treaties with the UK which give UK tax exemption on a pension received from a foreign country. It is always worth checking therefore whether the amount received is fully taxable in the United Kingdom or whether there is any tax relief or exemption due because of the terms of an existing treaty with the country concerned.

· 4 ·
TRADE, PROFESSION OR VOCATION

Whereas those in employment are taxed to Schedule E, those who carry on a trade, profession or vocation are taxed under Schedule D. Though the rates of tax are identical, the method of taxation and the deductions which may be claimed are very different. Form 11 is likely to be the tax return which has been sent to people who are known to be carrying on a trade, profession or vocation.

	Income: 6 April 1987 to 5 April 1988			
	Trade, profession or vocation		Self	Wife
17-19	Business name and address	Type of income	£	£
		Enterprise allowance	£	£
20		Balancing charges	£	£
		Deductions for Capital Allowances	£	£
21	Deduction for Class 4 National Insurance Contributions enter 'X' here		▶ ☐	
	If your profits for Class 4 National Insurance Contributions purposes are affected by interest paid, certain capital allowances or losses not given in the assessment, give details on a separate sheet and enter 'X' here		▶ ☐	

Box 17 to 19
Here should be entered the nature of the trade or business and the address and the business name if it is different from that of the taxpayer himself. The profits to be entered are those for the period of account which ended in the year covered by the tax return. If accounts are made up to 31st December, then the relevant profits for the 1988/89 tax return are those between 1st January and 31st December 1987. If the business was started during the year to 5th April 1988 but accounts are for the twelve months ending 31st December 1988 then the only entry that is required on the tax return is the statement that the business was started on 1st January 1988 and the words 'profits to be agreed'.

Unless the period of account coincides with the beginning of the tax year on 5th April it will not be possible to include a figure for profit on the current year's tax return and that will be included on the following year's return. The usual entry at this part of the tax return for the self-employed is 'profits per accounts'. This is of course on the assumption that accounts are separately sent to the Revenue. They are happy with this entry so long as the accounts are submitted in reasonable time.

HOW TO ARRIVE AT PROFITS
Those in employment are simply taxed on the amount that they receive in the year, with some adjustment sometimes being made for money earned in the year but not received until a later year. Those who are self-employed are taxed on a completely different basis. Accounts are drawn up showing the income for a twelve-month period which can end on any date in the year, though it is convenient to take the last day of a month. From the income of the period – which includes amounts invoiced but not yet received – are deducted expenses which are '*WHOLLY AND EXCLUSIVELY INCURRED IN THE PERFORMANCE OF THAT TRADE PROFESSION OR VOCATION*'. The expenditure does not have to be productive so that expenses incurred on a business trip in the hope of obtaining new contracts which proved abortive will still be acceptable. Having deducted all the allowable expenses you arrive at a profit figure. This is the item which is of interest to the Revenue and this sum should go down on the tax return in the profits box.

Usually in a continuing business the assessment of tax due is based on the amount earned in the year up to a date ending in the previous tax year. Therefore in 1988/89 you would be taxed on the profit you would have made, say, up to 31st December 1987. The year to 31st December 1988 will be taxed in 1989/90 and so on. This rule differs only for the opening and the closing years of a trade, profession or vocation. Special adjustments required for these periods are set out below.

ENTERPRISE ALLOWANCE
For up to 52 weeks £40 per week is paid to assist unemployed people in setting up their own businesses. Payments since 17th March 1986 are chargeable not as the profits of a trade but

TRADE, PROFESSION OR VOCATION

separately under Schedule D, Case VI. This means that they should be shown separately on the tax return in the box provided and not included as part of the profits of a business. This will prevent them from being taxed more than once in the early years of a business.

Box 20 *BALANCING CHARGES*
If capital allowances have been claimed (see below) on assets used for a trade, it is possible that the asset in question may be sold. If the capital allowances expenditure pool then brought forward is less than the amount received, a balancing charge will arise and when received this amount is taxable. If expenditure is incurred on new assets then there will be no balancing charge and the asset sold will simply reduce the amount of capital allowances which will arise for that year. Examples of this are given below.

CAPITAL ALLOWANCES
Spending on assets which qualify for capital allowances is added to the capital allowances pool, and writing-down (depreciation) allowances are given on the qualifying expenditure in the pool for that year. The amount of the capital allowances claimed should be shown.

A typical profit calculation would therefore show:

Assessable profit 1988/89

Profit for year to 31 December 1987 ....£15,000

Plus balancing charge £1,000

Less capital allowances £3,000

Profit assessable 1988/89 ....£13,000

Box 21 *CLASS 4 NATIONAL INSURANCE CONTRIBUTIONS*
Those who are self-employed are liable for Class 2 National Insurance contributions (their self-employed stamp), and in

addition Class 4 National Insurance contributions which are subject to minimum levels of profits.

The rate for Class 4 on profits or gains between £4,590 and £15,340 is 6.3 per cent for the 1987/88 tax year and the same rate is applicable on the profits or gains between £4,450 and £14,820 for the 1986/87 tax year. Fifty per cent of the final settled amount of Class 4 National Insurance contributions that the trader is liable to pay for the year of assessment is deductable from taxable income for the year. Therefore if Class 4 National Insurance contributions are paid there should be a cross entered in the box next to Box 21 to obtain the deductions.

OPENING YEARS OF BUSINESS

The normal basis of assessment for a continuing source of self-employment is that of the preceding year. In the opening years there can be no preceding year basis and therefore special rules are used. These are:

● First year of assessment taxes the amount earned from the date of starting the business to the following 5th April.
● Second year of assessment taxes the amount earned in the first twelve months.
● Third year of assessment taxes the amount earned in the twelve months ending on an accounting date in the previous year.
● Fourth year of assessment taxes the amount earned for a twelve-month period of account ending in the previous year, and so on.

Example 1 shows how this works in practice. As the example shows, anything which happens in the first twelve months has a significant effect on the profits for the first three years and if it is possible to claim a deduction in the first twelve months rather than in the second the benefit obtained is always at least doubled and sometimes trebled, depending on the exact date in the year to which the accounts are drawn up. Quite a useful ploy therefore is to set up a business with another person, such as your wife, and engage her as an employee for the first twelve months so that her salary would count as a deduction from the profits. At the end of twelve months your employee can be taken into partnership and with a continuation election for the basis of

TRADE, PROFESSION OR VOCATION

assessment significant tax savings can accrue. This is shown by Example 2.

Example 1

Profits for first 12 months to 31.12.86= £12,000
Assessments first year 1985/86 actual basis $\frac{1}{4} \times 12,000$ = 3,000
1986/87 First 12 months = 12,000
1987/88 Previous year (PY) basis = 12,000
1988/89 will be based on profits for 12 months to 31.12.87 (PY basis)
1989/90 will be based on profits for 12 months to 31.12.88 (PY basis)

Example 2

(a) Wife as partner sharing profits 50:50 with husband
Profits £24,000 first year to 30.4.86

Assessments on partnership	**£**
1985/86 11/12 × 24,000	= 22,000
1986/87 First 12 months	= 24,000
1987/88 PY basis	= 24,000
Total =	70,000

(b) Wife as employee earning £12,000 in first year therefore
profit £24,000 minus wages £12,000= £12,000

Assessment on partnership	**£**
1985/86 11/12 × 12,000	= 11,000
1986/87 First 12 months	= 12,000
1987/88 PY basis	= 12,000
Total =	35,000
Plus taxed on wife to PAYE =	12,000
	47,000

i.e. profits of £70,000 − £47,000 = £23,000 are not taxed when wife is initially shown as employee.

CAPITAL ALLOWANCES

A deduction may be claimed against the profits assessable for a trade, profession or vocation for capital expenditure in the execution of that trade. Capital allowances are currently at the rate of 25 per cent per annum on a reducing balance basis. For example, assuming that capital allowances were originally due on the sum of £10,000, allowances will be given on the following basis:

Capital Expenditure	£10,000
25% writing-down allowance	£2,500
Balance carried forward	£7,500
Year 2: Capital allowances brought forward	£7,500
25% writing-down allowance	£1,875
Pool carried forward	£5,625
Year 3: Pool brought forward	£5,625
25% writing-down allowance	£1,406
Pool carried forward	£4,219

Capital allowances may continue to be claimed while the trade continues whether or not the asset involved has been sold. This method of claiming capital allowances on a reducing balance means that it can take eight years to claim ninety per cent of the capital expenditure and is a far cry from the method of allowances that were available on 100 per cent of capital expenditure prior to April 1984. It is possible to accelerate the allowances on assets which have a short life – for example computers – over a four-year period.

BALANCING CHARGES AND BALANCING ALLOWANCES

It may well be that the 25 per cent reducing balance method means that the value of the asset as shown by the capital allowances pool is either too great or too small compared with its actual market value. If therefore the asset is sold at the end of a trade there is a method of ensuring that there is a balancing allowance or balancing charge depending on the value of that asset. If, for example, an asset has a brought-forward figure of £3,000 and it is sold eventually for £4,000 there will be a balancing charge added to the profits of £1,000. If conversely it is sold for £2,000, a final balancing allowance of £1,000 will be given.

ASSETS QUALIFYING FOR CAPITAL ALLOWANCES

Capital allowances are due on assets which are used wholly and exclusively for the purposes of a trade, profession or vocation. These include all fixtures and fittings together with plant and machinery. The type of assets which would be allowed are:

Aerials
Aeroplanes
Air compressors and services
Air conditioning
Air lines
Bakery equipment
Bells
Bicycles
Blinds, curtains, blind boxes
  and pelmets
Boats
Boiler plants
Books
Brick kilns
Burglar alarms
Cameras
Canteen fittings and equipment
Cash dispensers
Central dictation equipment
Central heating systems
Cinema projection equipment
Clock installations

Computers
Cooking equipment
Cooling water systems
Counters and fittings
Crane gantries
Cupboards
Curtain rails, curtains and
  pelmets
Dentists' chairs
Desks
Disposal units
Drinking water fittings
Dry docks
Dumbwaiters
Dust extraction equipment
Electrically operated doors
Electrically operated roller
  shutters
Electrical wiring closely related
  to an accepted piece of plant
Electrical installations, e.g.
  special lighting systems, signs,

switchgear
Electrical scoring equipment
Emergency lighting
Escalators
Extinguishers
Fans
Fire alarms and systems
Fires (gas and electric)
Fire safety to comply with the
  requirements of the fire
  authority
Fitted desks, writing tables and
  screens
Floodlighting
Flooring, e.g. carpets
Furniture including beds,
  tables, chairs
Garage equipment
Generators
Gymnasium equipment
Hand driers
Heating installations, fittings,
  etc
Helicopters
Hoses and hose reels
Hovercrafts
Immersion and instant water
  heaters
Incinerators
Internal signs
Kitchen equipment
Laundry equipment
Letterboxes
Lift systems
Light fittings and lamps (if
  specialised for business)
Lightning conductors
Loose floor coverings and

doormats
Loose furniture
Mechanical doors, sliding
  doors, shutters etc
Mechanical hand dryers
Mechanical ventilation systems
Mechanical vehicle barriers
Mirrors
Movable partitions
Murals (if for ambience of
  guests, e.g. hotel)
Nameplates
Office equipment
Paper shredders
Passenger lifts and doors
Personnel call systems
Pictures (if for ambience of
  guests, e.g. hotel)
Plant rooms
Power cables (not ordinary
  mains)
Power installations
Public address and piped
  music fittings
Pumps, e.g. water, petrol
Quarantine premises
Racking, cupboards
  (removable)
Radio, television and data
  transmission installations
Refrigeration installations
Refuse collection and disposal
  systems
Safes, night safe and enclosures
Safety equipment, screens etc
Sanitary installations
Sauna and jacuzzi, e.g. for
  health farm

Screens in a window display (movable)
Sculptures (for creating ambience)
Security devices
Shelving
Shopfronts on a renewals basis
Showers and baths
Shutters
Smoke detectors and heat detectors
Soft furnishings
Software purchased at the same time as the computer
Software with a life of more than two years
Special acoustic ceilings
Special foundations or reinforced flooring for plant
Special housing around plant
Special lighting related to the trade
Sprinkler systems
Squash court surfaces
Standby supply system
Storage racks
Storage tanks
Strong room doors
Swimming pools directly related to trading activities,
e.g. holiday camp
Switchboards
Switchgear
Tapestries (for creating ambience)
Telephone systems and conduits
Television installations (including aerials)
Telex and fax machines
Towel dispensers
Towel rails
Transformers
Turntables
Underfloor heating
Vehicles
Ventilation equipment
Video equipment
WC partitions (if demountable)
Wall decor (for creating ambience)
Wash basins including drains etc
Water heaters
Water treatment and filtration equipment
Window panels, lighting and sockets for a shop front
Wiring to plant, e.g. smoke detectors

This list gives examples of the assets which might qualify and is not intended to be an exhaustive list. The theme running through it is that the assets must either be chattels or fixtures which do not form part of the structure of the premises and which have a function in the business. This functional test has been held to give capital allowances on the swimming pool used by a holiday camp or the canopy over a petrol station forecourt. It was ruled, however, that a boat used as a floating restaurant did not qualify since the boat itself was held to be the premises within which the restaurant trade was taking place. In recent years court cases have decided that capital allowances can extend in very specific circumstances to the pictures, ornaments and other sculptures used to give ambience in a hotel group but a claim for capital allowances on pictures to brighten up an accountant's reception area would probably fail as it would be held that ambience was not so important to his profession.

It is sometimes possible to split items of expenditure: in a squash court case it was held that the structure of the building itself was capital with no allowances being due but the specialised surface put on to the basic structure in order to turn it into a functioning squash court was allowable, as that did serve a function.

SPECIAL CAPITAL ALLOWANCES

The notes above have dealt with the main capital allowances. It must also be remembered, however, that there are other specialised allowances for items such as hotels, know-how, scientific research, mineral depletion and industrial buildings.

INDUSTRIAL BUILDINGS ALLOWANCES

Industrial buildings allowances are generally due on buildings used for the purposes of a qualifying trade which means either a manufacturing trade or one which processes or repairs items. The normal rate of allowances is 4 per cent per annum on a flat basis for 25 years until the 100 per cent expenditure on the building itself (but not the land) has been recovered.

There are provisions to carry forward the original expenditure to a purchaser so that they may also enjoy the capital expenditure over the balance of the original 25-year period. This means, therefore, that if there is expenditure of £100,000 on a building, allowances of £4,000 per annum may be claimed over the 25-year period. If after 15 years the building is sold for £200,000, then the original £100,000 exenditure may be claimed by the purchaser at £10,000 per year over ten years. The vendor, who has already enjoyed capital allowances on the building of some £60,000, is taxed on a balancing charge of this amount in the year when he makes his disposal.

EXPENDITURE IN ENTERPRISE ZONES

There is one specialised class of allowances for expenditure on industrial buildings in enterprise zones of which there are some 26 around the country, for example Swansea, Corby, Docklands, Chatham Dockyards or Tyneside. Expenditure in these zones on buildings, other than a dwelling house, which are let commercially entitle the person who either incurs the expenditure or who purchases an unused building in the zone to claim 100 per cent industrial buildings allowances in the year that the expenditure is incurred. As an alternative a 25 per cent writing-down allowance may be taken over a four-year period.

A summary of the capital allowances which may be claimed is shown in the table below.

CAPITAL ALLOWANCES

Type	Rate	Method
Plant & machinery	25% p.a.	Reducing balance
Industrial buildings allowance	4% p.a.	Straight line
Enterprise zone "	100% p.a.	
	or 25% p.a.	Straight line
Qualifying hotels	4% p.a.	Straight line
Scientific research	100%	
Agricultural buildings allowance	4% p.a.	Straight line
Know-how	25% p.a.	Reducing balance
Mines, oil wells	10% p.a.	Reducing balance
	or 25% p.a.	do.
Patent rights	25% p.a.	Reducing balance
Short life assets	25% p.a.	Reducing balance separate pool
Expensive (> £8,000) cars	25% p.a. limit £2,000	Reducing balance

Sales of assets for more than the tax written-down value will result in a clawback of all or part of the tax allowances received – a balancing charge.

Sale of assets for less than the tax written-down value will result in an additional balancing allowance.

· 5 ·
PROPERTY

Anyone who has a large income from letting property should
certainly read the Inland Revenue leaflet IR27 which indicates not
only what is taxable, but also what allowances may be claimed.
Property is divided into the following categories:

	Property in the UK		Gross income including premiums	Expenses (enclose statement)	Self	Wife
	*delete as appropriate	Address				
25	*Unfurnished lettings		£	£	£	£
	*Furnished lettings					
	*Furnished holiday					
26	lettings					
	*Ground rents or					
27	Feu duties					
	*Land					

Box 25   UNFURNISHED LETTINGS
These are taxable under Schedule A and you should include on
the tax returns the income received in the year up to 5th April. All
the normal outgoings may be claimed against the letting income
including agents' fees, repairs, rent, utilities, insurance and so on.
The amount left after these deductible items is taxed on an actual
basis as it arises. The Revenue normally issue an initial assessment
based upon the income of the previous year until details of the
income for the current year are known. It is best to include a list
of the actual expenses claimed against the gross income as a
schedule accompanying the tax return. It should be noted that
interest on money borrowed is not an allowable deduction
against the unfurnished letting income, although it may be
claimed elsewhere.

FURNISHED LETTINGS
Furnished lettings are usually taxed under Case VI of Schedule D
and are treated differently to unfurnished lettings in that capital
allowances may be claimed against the cost of the furniture.
These may either be claimed on the renewals basis where no
deduction is given for the cost of the original furniture but
renewals are given in full so long as there is no improvement
element, or on the far better basis of 10 per cent of the net rent
(equivalent to the gross rent of the property less the rates paid by

the landlord). This 10 per cent may be claimed each year whether there has been any additional expenditure on furniture or not and is a concessional allowance granted by the Revenue.

Many people attempt to have furnished lettings or unfurnished lettings taxed as if they are a trade, especially if they have a large number of properties and provide a range of services. While in the past the Revenue would accept this treatment, they would now contest any attempt to treat the item as a trade even if the income has been taxed as trading income for many years in the past. This is particularly relevant when it comes to claiming retirement relief or rollover relief (see pages 37 and 124) on any capital gains on disposal of the property. The Revenue view is that such reliefs are not available except in the case of furnished holiday lettings.

FURNISHED HOLIDAY LETTINGS

These should be shown separately from the other furnished property and in general letting qualifies as holiday letting where:

● The property is available for letting to the public on a commercial basis as holiday accommodation for not less than 140 days.
● It is usually let commercially as holiday accommodation for at least seventy days, and
● For at least seven months of the year it is not in the same occupation for a continuous period of more than 31 days.

Furnished holiday lettings occupy a privileged position in that they are treated as a deemed trade if all the above conditions are satisfied and therefore both rollover benefit and retirement relief are due. In addition any interest commitments may be claimed as a direct deduction against the income of the deemed trade.

In general any sale of property which has been let will be liable to Capital Gains Tax. If property has been bought and sold quickly without any letting it is possible for the Revenue to argue that any profits are liable to Income Tax. This section of the tax return should also include any income from letting caravans, garages or indeed furnished or unfurnished rooms in your own home. If the rooms are in your house or are part of a property which has at one time been your private residence, when the property is sold there are significant Capital Gains Tax reliefs available up to the limit of either the personal Capital Gains Tax exemption relating to your period of occupation as a residence or £20,000, whichever is the lesser.

Box 26   *GROUND RENT OR FEU DUTIES*

If there is any income of this kind it should simply be recorded. There are unlikely to be any expenses to claim against the ground rent or feu duties received.

Box 27   *LAND*

Income from land is taxed under Schedule A and the address of any furnished or unfurnished property should be entered together with the full amount of the rent due for the year. You should note that it is the amount due for the year on which you are taxed and not the amount you receive. This is a principle of Schedule A taxation. If eventually the amount due is not received it is possible to reduce the assessment to the amount actually received, especially when there has been a formal waiver.

GENERAL

It is often thought that if you own property in say, Cardiff, and live in London then you may claim the cost of travelling to that property against the rental income. This is something which the Revenue contests in almost all cases since the cost of travelling to Cardiff is because of the landlord's personal circumstances and not a consequence of letting the property. The expenses which may be claimed are the normal running costs and not those peculiar to your own personal circumstances.

· 6 ·
DIVIDENDS AND INTEREST

Box 29   UK INTEREST NOT TAXED BEFORE RECEIPT

National Savings Bank
Seventy pounds of the total interest from the ordinary deposit account with the National Savings Bank is exempt from tax. A wife may also claim £70 exemption against her income from such accounts. All interest should, however, be included and the Revenue will allow any exemption due. Certain items, such as terminal bonuses under the Government-approved Save As You Earn scheme, are not taxable and need not be entered on the tax return. All income from the investment account and deposit income bonds is taxable in full.

Box 30   OTHER BANK DEPOSITS
There should now be comparatively few bank accounts which pay interest on which tax has not been deducted at source under the composite rate tax (CRT) scheme. If interest has been received from such a source then this should be entered here, giving the name of the bank.

Box 31
This will include all interest on which tax has not been deducted at source nor already returned under Box 29 and 30. It can cover items such as war loan, British Savings Bonds or money lent to your own family, for which there would of course be no tax deducted at source but on which the interest is most definitely taxable. If you have purchased a Certificate of Tax Deposit the interest on it is taxable unless the Certificate has been surrendered by way of a settlement on a Revenue investigation case, when it is set against the interest that would otherwise be due to the Revenue.
    The following are not taxable:
- Accumulated interest on National Savings Certificates.
- Ulster Savings Certificates.

● Interest awarded by a United Kingdom court as part of an award for damages for personal injury or death.

Interest received which is not taxed before receipt is taxed under Case III of Schedule D. The basis of assessment is that in the first year of the source you are taxed on the actual amount received. This is also the case in the second year of the source, but in the third and succeeding years you are taxed on the amount received in the preceding year until the source comes to an end, when for the last and penultimate year you are again taxed on the actual amount received.

There are slight variations to this general rule: in the third year of assessment the taxpayer may if he wishes elect to be taxed on the basis of the current year rather than the preceding year if the amount received is less than in the preceding year. If the interest ceases, the final year is taxed on an actual basis and the preceding year can at the Revenue's option be increased to the actual amount if that is greater than the figure already taxed on the preceding year basis.

Box 32 *UNTAXED INCOME FROM ABROAD*

This is taxed either under Case IV or Case V of Schedule D. For those who are non-UK domiciled (see pages 34 and 35) or for British subjects or citizens of the Republic of Ireland who are not ordinarily resident in the United Kingdom taxation is on the remittance basis – if money is earned on deposit accounts abroad but not remitted to the United Kingdom then no tax will be due. For those who are domiciled and resident in the United Kingdom, or for those British subjects or citizens of the Republic of Ireland who are ordinarily resident, the basis of taxation is on the arising basis, that is, on money that has been paid or credited to them, so that any amounts earned on deposit accounts or other investment income abroad are taxed in the UK whether they are brought here or not.

Taxation under Case IV and Case V of Schedule D is generally based on the actual amount arising in the first two years. Assessment for the third year is based on the previous year, subject to the right of election that if the actual income arising in the third year is less than that assessed on the previous year, then tax can be based on that current year. When the source of income ceases, tax for the final year is always based on the actual amount arising, while the assessment for the penultimate year is increased to the actual amount arising if this is greater than the figure for the previous year.

The amount to be shown on the tax return is the actual amount of any foreign income which has not been taxed in the United Kingdom. The full amount arising in the year to 5th April should be returned whether or not it was received in the United Kingdom. If, however, you are relying on the exemption referred to above for non-UK domiciles and non-resident British subjects then you can simply make a note that no amount was remitted to the United Kingdom in that particular year so that no taxation arises, without including details of what the amounts were.

You are allowed to claim expenses against income which has been earned abroad. An example of this is rental income arising from letting a foreign property, such as a Spanish villa. You would be allowed to claim for the various management expenses, the charges and repairs associated with the normal letting of property. There is no way, however, in which you can obtain relief for any interest paid on a loan raised to acquire foreign property. Because the income arises under Case V of Schedule D there is no interest relief, whereas there would have been if the same property had been let in the UK.

The difference between Case IV and Case V of Schedule D is academic these days, but in general Case IV relates to overseas Government securities, whereas Case V covers all other forms of foreign possessions including bank accounts, property, and overseas professions.

It is quite possible that foreign tax will have been charged on income arising abroad. If this is the case it is usually possible to claim full or partial double taxation relief on the amount of foreign tax charged as against the amount of tax that would be due on the same income in the UK. More details of this are given in the comments on Box 39, page 63.

Income: 6 April 1987 to 5 April 1988		
Interest treated as taxed before receipt (Composite Rate Tax)		
33 Interest from UK banks and deposit takers taxed before receipt	Self	Wife
Name of bank or deposit taker	£	£
33 Interest from UK building societies		
Name of society	£	£

Box 33 *INTEREST TAXED BEFORE RECEIPT*

Bank or deposit taker

Since 5th April 1985 banks and deposit takers, including the Bank of England and Post Office (but not the National Savings Bank), operate the composite rate scheme when paying interest to depositors. This means that the interest received has had basic rate tax deducted at source. If you are taxable only at the basic rate there is no further tax due on the sums involved. But for those who are not taxable in full on the amounts received there is no possibility of obtaining a repayment of any tax deducted at source. Amounts received are taxed on an actual basis and the figure to be entered on the tax return is the amount actually received which will be the net sum after the basic rate tax has been deducted. If you are liable to pay a higher rate of tax the Revenue will gross up the sum involved.

Accordingly, if you have received £73 interest in the year to 5th April this will be regarded as £100 gross, so that at the maximum 60 per cent rate of tax you would be expected to pay an additional £33 on the amount received. When taken off the £73 you actually received, this would result in a net receipt of £40. This equates to 60 per cent tax on the gross of £100. It is the grossed-up interest which is included in any computation of taxable income, for example in working out entitlement to age allowance.

If interest has been received from a bank which was not taxed at source then this should be returned under Box 30.

Building societies

Building societies and banks are now very much in the same category when it comes to receipt of interest, so the comments on bank interest also apply to building societies and you should simply enter the net amount received from the building society. There is no way that tax deducted at source by the building society can be repaid to a depositor and people with allowance entitlements should therefore invest where interest is paid gross.

36	Dividends from UK companies and tax credits	Amount of dividend	Amount of tax credit
	Name of UK company		
	Self	£	£
	Wife	£	£

37-40	Other dividends, trust income, etc, already taxed	Gross amount of income
	Name of source (show each separately)	
	Self	£
	Wife	£

Box 36   DIVIDENDS FROM UNITED KINGDOM COMPANIES AND TAX CREDITS

All dividends paid by United Kingdom companies to their shareholders require the company to have deducted tax at source and to attach a voucher to the dividends certificate indicating that this tax is available as a tax credit to the shareholder in the company. If therefore the company declares a dividend in 1987/88 of £73 they will pay to the Inland Revenue advance Corporation Tax of £27 and will provide the shareholder with a certificate declaring that they have received a dividend of £73 plus tax credit of £27. The recipient will be treated as having received gross income of £100 on which tax of £27 has already been paid. If he is liable for tax at basic rate only, no more tax is due, but if he is liable at higher rates of tax up to another £33 may be charged, as is the case with bank interest.

If the dividend were declared in 1988/89 the recipient would receive £75 plus a tax credit for £25. If liable to higher rate tax up to another £15 may be due, so that the total tax suffered would be £40 on the gross income of £100, equivalent to the maximum 40 per cent applicable in 1988/89.

The important difference between dividends and interest from a bank or building society is that the tax credit attached to the dividend is available for repayment if this might be due, perhaps because the taxpayer has excess personal allowances or might have made a relievable loss from another source in the same year.

Distributions which do not come with any tax credits, or if the voucher shows Income Tax deducted at source, should be returned in Box 37. Even if dividends are received from a private company there should still be a tax credit certificate. You are taxable in the year to which the dividend relates. For instance it is quite usual for a company to declare a dividend for the year to 31st December 1987 with the actual dividend being paid in May 1988. This would therefore be income for the 1988/89 tax year, so that it will be returned on the tax return for 1989/90.

HIGHER RATE TAX

Higher rate tax on dividends, building society and bank interest is due on the 1st December following the year to which it relates, so if the income is for the year 1987/88 the higher rate tax will be due on the 1st December 1988. There used to be an additional form of tax of 15 per cent over and above the highest rate of tax called investment income surcharge. This was abolished from 1984/85 onwards.

Box 37 **OTHER DIVIDENDS, INTEREST ALREADY TAXED**

This is where you should declare sources of income on which Income Tax has already been deducted, for example income from unit trusts including income re-invested in units if the voucher shows that Income Tax has been deducted. You should also return here any loan interest or mortgage interest taxed before receipt. This could, for instance, be loan interest received from a company which has deducted tax at source before making the interest payment.

Box 38   TRUST INCOME

This can be of many different sorts. Trusts in general are either known as discretionary settlements or as interest in possession settlements. If the latter applies then the beneficiary or beneficiaries are entitled to all the income of the trust and should therefore return the income of the trust as being theirs. If Peter and Paul are absolutely entitled in equal shares to all the income of the P & P settlement and that settlement receives income of £10,000 per year, then they should show £5,000 each as their entitlement. On making the payments to Peter and Paul the trust will provide a tax deduction certificate showing that the basic rate tax was deducted at source before payment was made.

A discretionary settlement is taxed at the basic rate plus an additional rate which gives a total of 45 per cent in 1987/88 and earlier years and of 35 per cent in 1988/89. Any income payments made to beneficiaries of the trust will provide tax deduction certificates showing the tax which has been deducted at source. Before 6th April 1988 this would be at 45 per cent, but any income payments made after 5th April 1988 will show tax at source of 35 per cent even though the trust itself may have suffered tax at the higher 45 per cent rate on the income which it is now distributing.

Anti-avoidance provisions with regard to trusts

The trusts set up by parents in favour of their minor children will not be effective for Income Tax purposes and all the income of the trust will be taxed on the parents. Similarly if the person who sets up the trust (the settlor) retains an interest in the income of the trust in some way, then all the income of that trust will continue to be treated as the income of the settlor, even if amounts are paid out to beneficiaries. These amounts will be treated effectively as gifts from the settlor.

Box 39   DOUBLE TAXATION RELIEF

If income arises abroad then, unless it is in a tax haven, it is quite possible that local taxes will be due or will have been deducted at source. This can apply to any income from earnings or investment. It is usual to be able to claim relief for the tax paid overseas against the United Kingdom tax due. Further information can be acquired from the local tax district but in general the UK taxation authorities will provide credit up to the equivalent of the UK tax which would be due. If, for example, UK tax of £30 would have been due on a particular receipt and overseas tax of £28 has already been paid, the UK will only levy the balance of £2. If on the other hand overseas tax of £32 has been paid, the UK will not seek any further tax but will not repay the £2 difference.

The UK has double taxation treaties with many overseas countries and it is often possible under these treaties to ensure that the foreign tax suffered is at a lower level than would have otherwise been the case. This can improve cash flow and may also reduce the total tax levied, though to the extent that the foreign tax would have been relieved against the UK tax bill there would be no overall difference.

Box 40 FOREIGN INCOME ALREADY TAXED IN THE UNITED KINGDOM

You should enter the full amount here (before deduction of overseas and UK income tax) of foreign income which has already been taxed in the UK. If tax has been charged at a rate other than the normal basic rate then this should be indicated.

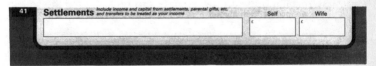

Box 41 SETTLEMENTS

This is where to show income from settlements which are to be treated as the income of the settlor either because he has retained an interest in the settlement or because the trust was by parents for minor children and the children have benefited from the income. It is also the place to show receipts of capital from settlements which will not be taxable on the recipient, although there may be some Inheritance Tax consequences to consider. Any parental gifts (which are generally not taxable) should also be shown in Box 41.

The term 'settlement' includes any disposition, trust, covenant agreement or arrangement including parental gifts to unmarried children under the age of eighteen. If any of the following conditions apply the income of the settlement may be taxed as the settlor's:

● The settlement is for a period which cannot exceed six years or if to a charity then the period cannot exceed three years.
● The capital or income from the settlement is paid to or otherwise benefits a minor child.
● The income arises from assets transferred to a child while the child is under the age of eighteen and unmarried.
● The settlor or his wife may at some time benefit from income or capital from the settlement either by the exercise of some power or otherwise.

These provisions can also apply if income is accumulated in the settlement and payment is made as capital sums or loans to the settlor or his wife by the trustees. Though transfer of income to a charity will mean that it is not treated as that of the covenantor for all purposes, that is, there will be higher-rate tax relief, payments made under a Deed of Covenant only obtain basic rate relief and the donor continues to be liable for the higher rates of tax.

Income: 6 April 1987 to 5 April 1988			
42	Payments from estates *Include receipts from the estates of deceased persons in Administration*	Self	Wife
		£	£

Box 42 *PAYMENTS FROM DECEASED PERSONS' ESTATES*
The recipient should enter the name of the deceased person, the date of death and the name of the executor or person who represents the administrator of the estate. Payments are normally

made to named beneficiaries by the personal representative of the deceased before they have actually sorted out who gets what under the will. Normally when payments are made basic rate tax will have been deducted at source. Sometimes if the beneficiary is the sole inheritor and is therefore entitled to all the income under the estate it is permissable to pay all income directly to him or her so long as it is entered in the beneficiary's tax return. This point should be clarified with the Revenue before the return is made.

· 7 ·
OTHER PROFITS OR INCOME

This is the section of the tax return where you should declare any income which does not seem to find a place elsewhere.

43-51	**All other profits or income** *enter gross amounts*		Self	Wife
	Maintenance, alimony, or aliment received		£	£
	Any other income not entered elsewhere eg: accrued income charges and taxable gains on life assurance policies		£	£

Box 43 INCOME RECEIVABLE BY A COMPANY OR TRUST ABROAD

Income which arises under one of the Revenue's anti-avoidance sections should be entered here. It applies where the ability to earn income has been transferred to a person (including a company or a trust) resident abroad. For example, at its simplest, if £10,000 is transferred to a company in Jersey, and that company received £1,000 per year interest, then the person who transferred the £10,000 should show on his or her tax return the £1,000 income enjoyed by the Jersey company. This could also be the case if income of that company was much greater than £1,000 because it had other income as well, for instance if it had traded with the £10,000 received. In certain circumstances the whole income of the company is theoretically taxed upon the transferor. If any benefit has been received from the overseas person, such as a holiday which may have been paid for by the overseas company, then that benefit should be returned in Box 43.

There is an overriding provision that the section will not apply if it can be shown that avoidance of tax was not a purpose of the transfer of assets and any associated operations. There have been recent developments in tax law, however, which have shown that even undertaking an employment with an overseas company for no or low remuneration could be within the terms of this anti-avoidance section, so that you would be obliged to return all the income of the company as your own.

Box 44   TRANSFER OF INCOME FROM SECURITIES

If you have sold or transferred the right to receive dividends or interest without also disposing of the securities the dividends and interest are treated as your income for tax purposes. Any such transfers of income should be returned in Box 44. If the shares have actually been sold then there is no requirement to return the income.

Box 45   FUNDING BONDS

If instead of arrears of interest the taxpayer has received funding bonds including stocks, shares, securities or certificates of indebtedness from any source, then a return should be made since the value of the holdings received is taxable in the same way as the arrears of interest would have been.

Box 46   RECEIPTS AFTER CESSATION OF A TRADE, PROFESSION OR VOCATION

It is often the case that some time after a trade, profession or vocation has ceased income is received. This is particularly apposite in the case of royalties which may be received many years after an author has abandoned his profession. Such profits cannot be taxed as part of the trade, profession or vocation but must be treated separately and taxed under Case VI of Schedule D. Any expenses subsequently incurred can be set against this income.

It is always possible for the Revenue to tax income after the trade, profession or vocation has ceased, but if there is no income, a post-cessation expense is not relieved in any way. It is also possible to elect that instead of income being taxed when received it should be treated as received on the last day of the trade, profession or vocation. This would allow a trading loss arising at that time to be set against it.

Box 47   SALE OF PATENT RIGHTS

If patent rights have been sold for a capital sum Income Tax may be due on the amounts received. Full details should be given at this part of the tax return so that the Revenue may decide on the tax position. Any sum receivable by a UK resident is assessable under Schedule D, Case VI. The amount is spread equally over the year of receipt and the five succeeding years, or if a written election is made within two years it may be wholly charged in the year of receipt.

Box 48

If capital allowances (see page 43) have been claimed for an asset used other than for a trade, profession or vocation, such as an industrial building let as an investment, and that asset is disposed of, a balancing charge may arise if the amount received on sale is greater than the tax written-down value. In such cases details of the balancing charge should be shown in Box 48 and the balancing charge will be taxable under Case VI of Schedule D.

Box 49   *WOODLANDS*

Until 6th April 1988 woodlands were taxed to their own unique basis called Schedule B. This taxed the owner on the occupation of woodlands in the United Kingdom managed on a commercial basis with the purpose of making a profit. Tax was not based at all upon the income from the timber but was one third of the woodlands' annual value – in effect one third of the gross rateable value of the bare land, ignoring the trees. This could mean tax on as little as 15p per acre. But instead of being taxed to Schedule B, until 15th March 1988 woodland owners could elect to be assessed under Schedule D. This treats the woodland as a trade. The advantages were that in the first fifteen years or so of the life of a wood the amount of expenditure on planting, repairs, insurance, drainage, husbandry and so on far outweigh the income which might arise, so losses were created. If an election had been made to be taxed under Schedule D then these losses could be relieved against other income so that if, for example, someone has made a £10,000 loss in planting trees, and has other income of, say, £100,000 per year, then the £10,000 can be taken off the £100,000. The recipient is therefore taxed only on £90,000, obtaining relief at 1987/88 tax rates of up to 60 per cent on the £10,000 loss.

Once taxed under Schedule D the taxpayer was charged in full on any sales of trees. It was therefore quite a common ploy that before the profitable years started, 12 to 13 years in the case of softwoods or 15 to 50 years in the case of hardwoods, the woodland would either be sold with the consequence indicated below or there would be a transfer from the taxpayer to his wife or child or to some other relative. They would not elect for the Schedule D basis but rather were taxed to Schedule B so that they only had to pay the insignificant amounts indicated above, despite the fact that the land might well be producing £10,000 to £30,000 per annum.

There are also tax advantages when it came to selling woodlands in that there is no Capital Gains Tax on the value of the trees whether standing or fallen and the only capital gains which arose was on the increase in the bare value of the land. Effectively, therefore, you could build up a Capital Gains Tax free asset out of tax allowances against other income.

In case these tax advantages were not sufficient to tempt the wealthy into investing in woodlands, the Forestry Commission also provides grants to encourage planting of both softwood and hardwood trees.

Woodland was the granddaddy of all tax avoidance schemes but despite its ancient pedigree the advantages have been removed for all new investors from 15th March 1988. Following the abolition of Schedule B, it will not be possible for those who invest in commercial woodlands to elect for this Schedule D treatment. This means that their losses cannot be relieved against other income. There will be some compensation in that the grants paid by the Forestry Commission to those who plant trees were also increased at the same time as the Income Tax advantages were removed. The Capital Gains Tax advantages remain and so do those of Inheritance Tax. The value of woodland can be discounted by up to 50 per cent of its actual value if the land has been owned for a sufficient period, which can be as short as two years. Those who own valuable commercial woodlands therefore gain a very significant relief against Inheritance Tax. The absurdity of the previous Forestry investment advantages can be shown by the fact that despite the abolition of Schedule B the tax yield to the Revenue from such a change is expected to increase by ten million pounds per year.

Transitional provisions

Tax relief under the existing rules will continue to be available until 5th April 1993 for those who are already occupiers of commercial woodlands. The relief is also available until 5th April 1993 for those who become occupiers as a result of commitments entered into or applications for grants received by the Forestry Commission before 15th March 1988. Occupiers of commercial woodlands who will benefit from the transitional reliefs will also be entitled to claim the higher planting allowances, but will not be entitled to claim loss relief on the same expenditure.

Box 50 **STOCK DIVIDENDS**

Any stock dividend issued by a company is treated as taxed income of the recipient. The payment of the stock dividend is instead of a cash dividend. The only liability is to higher rate tax, but no allowance will be made against the basic rate tax which will already have been paid. The shareholder is treated as receiving the shares on the due date of issue, that is the earliest date the compay is required to issue them. For Capital Gains Tax purposes stock dividends received are deemed to be acquired for a consideration equal to the relevant cash dividend or market value and treated as a rights issue taken up.

Box 51 **ANY OTHER INCOME NOT ENTERED ELSEWHERE**

There are many other forms of income which come within this category and the list below is therefore not meant to be exhaustive but rather illustrative. All the income concerned is taxable under Schedule D.

1. Profit from isolated or artistic activities

2. Casual earnings These might result from writing a weekly column for a periodical. Any such income if it does not amount to a profession is taxed under Case VI. Casual earnings can cover items such as the odd secretarial job or serving behind the bar in a pub or picking hops on a farm in the summer. If the amounts involved have not been taxed to PAYE, they should be returned under Case VI of Schedule D.

3. *Alimony or maintenance payments* The 1988 Budget completely reformed the alimony and maintenance payments regime. Maintenance arrangements made from 15th March 1988 are within the new rules so that the recipient is not taxable on the amount received. Payments under existing arrangements at 15th March 1988 continue under the old rules except that the first £1,490 of the amount received is not taxed. The effect of the rules is shown by the following examples comparing the effects of the new and old rules:

Example 1

Divorced husband pays his ex-wife £100 per month (£1,200 per year)

Ex-wife taxable on:

Present Rules £1,200
Pre 15.3.88 Court orders . . . . Nil
(Maintenance is less than £1,490)
Post 15.3.88 Court orders . . . . Nil

Example 2

Divorced husband pays his ex-wife £150 per month (£1,800 per year)

Ex-wife taxable on:

Present Rules £1,800
Pre 15.3.88 Court orders £1,800
less £1,490
_____
£310
Post 15.3.88 Court orders . . . . Nil

---

These new rules apply to amounts received in 1988/89 but the old system is relevant with regard to the 1988/89 tax return which covers income to 5th April 1988, so it is very important to understand the old rules.

Alimony is received with tax having been deducted at source and therefore the gross amount should be shown with an indication that tax was deducted. If instead the amounts received are 'small maintenance payments' then the amount actually received should be noted with an indication that no tax has been deducted. Voluntary payments are not returned in this section as they are not income of the recipient.

Small maintenance payments are payments made under a UK court order.

(a) By one party to a marriage or former marriage to or for the maintenance of the other party.

(b) To any person under 21 for his own benefit, maintenance, education.

(c) To any person for the benefit, maintenance or education of a person under 21.

The maximum payments under these categories are £48 per week or £208 per month for payment after 6th April 1986 under (a) and (b), payments under (c) are at the limit of £25 per week or £108 per month. Small maintenance payments for periods before 6th April 1989 are taxable to Case III of Schedule D, subject to the £1,490 exemption for 1988/89.

4. Gains on life assurance policies These are common and are not chargeable to Capital Gains Tax but rather to Income Tax. While the proceeds of most life assurance policies are free from tax there is some to pay if you are liable for tax at higher rates or would be so if the gain involved was added to your income, and either the policy is not a qualifying policy but is a single premium policy, or it is a qualifying policy but was cashed in early before the first ten years were up.

In general, the amounts charged under this section are the excess of the amount received over and above 5 per cent of the total paid in for each year since the previous receipt from the policy. When a policy comes to an end the gain is normally the amount received less the total premiums paid. The sums received are added to the taxable income and charged at a higher rate tax if any such liability arises.

In addition, gains on life annuity contracts starting after 26th March 1974 and any overseas life assurance policy taken out after 17th November 1983 are also chargeable at the basic rate. Generally, however, only higher rate liability can arise and there are provisions for giving top slicing relief if the rate of tax suffered by the maturity of one of these chargeable policies is atypical of the average tax rate that would have been due if the total gain had been divided by the number of years the policy had been in force.

5. Personal equity plans Withdrawals from a Personal Equity Plan may give rise to an Income Tax charge if not within the terms of the scheme. Amounts must be invested for a complete calendar year to avoid the charge.

6. Covenant income The regime for deeds of covenants, like maintenance payments, has undergone a radical change since 15th March 1988. From that date non-charitable convenants made by individuals will have no effect for tax purposes. This means that payments do not require to have tax deducted from them and the payer will therefore receive no tax relief. The recipient will not pay tax on them nor be able to claim repayment.

The rules governing charitable covenants are unchanged. The present rules continue to apply to all other convenants made by individuals by 15th March 1988 provided that they have been received by the tax office by 30th June 1988.

Apart from those to charities, most covenants are made by parents to their student children. Despite the fact that the Revenue themselves put out a student pack indicating how the covenants should be arranged, they do not now feel that covenants should be used for such a purpose. The parent has to go through the legal process of making a covenant and supplying evidence of payment on top of the usual need to report income to the local authority when applying for the student's grant. The

Revenue then have to check the student's income and repay him or her the tax that had been paid. As covenant income itself was taxable, many students were discouraged from taking holiday jobs for which they might be taxed because they might have used up their personal allowances against the covenant.

Under the new proposals all this is changed but, so that families with students at university will not feel the full impact, it is proposed to amend the parental contributions to student grants so that as the covenant relief is withdrawn, more grant income comes from the local authority rather than from the parent.

Income received under a Deed of Covenant has already had the basic rate tax deducted at source. If the total income of the recipient including the gross amount of the covenant payments puts him into the higher-rate tax band, further tax will be due, but if the total amount received is less than the personal allowances due then tax suffered under the covenant can be repaid.

7. Accrued income scheme If securities are transferred cum-dividend or securities have been transferred to the recipient ex-dividend, then there is a possibility of a charge to Income Tax arising on the income accrued on the securities. This was previously a useful ploy for converting income into capital gains which were taxable to a maximum rate of 30 per cent and also enjoy a high annual exemption.

8. Land Transactions Normally buying and selling of land will either be liable to Capital Gains Tax (see page 102) or be treated as trading. If, however, the transaction is not a capital gain but falls short of trading, then it can be liable under Case VI of Schedule D as being a purchase and sale of land with the sole main object of realising a gain from disposal. The type of transaction which may come within the Section would be where someone purchased a plot of land and developed it by obtaining planning permission, perhaps laying out roads and laying on services, and then arranged for the land to be sold off in plots to potential house purchasers. This may fall short of trading if the taxpayer had never done this type of activity before, neither would it be capital gains as the land was not bought with the intention of being held as an investment. The provisions of Case VI Schedule D would therefore apply so that the profits would be chargeable to Income Tax.

· 8 ·
OUTGOINGS

The first part of the tax return covers items on which you are taxed. The 'Outgoings' section is much nearer to people's hearts for included here is what you can claim as a deduction against taxable income.

	Outgoings: 6 April 1987 to 5 April 1988		
	Expenses in employment	Self	Wife
56	Details of expenses	£	£
57	Fees or subscriptions to professional bodies	*Name of professional body*	£	£

Box 56 *EXPENSES IN EMPLOYMENT*

Under tax law you may only claim against your employment those expenses which are '*wholly, exclusively and necessarily incurred in the necessary performance of one's duties*'. The term 'necessarily' is strictly applied and there may be many expenses which you might regard as a legitimate deduction from your earnings but which the Revenue will say are not necessarily incurred in the performance of your duties.

Examples of this strictness are the paging units which a doctor on call for kidney transplants might well require so that he can keep in touch at all times. Claims for expenditure on such a unit would, however, not be accepted because they were not incurred necessarily for the performance of the doctor's duties. Otherwise every other doctor in the same position must incur such an expenditure and if that were the case why did the medical authorities themselves not provide the unit?

Similarly, if a teacher attended a night school course in order to attain knowledge to impart to his pupils, he might regard that expenditure necessary in the performance of his duties. But the Revenue would again (with case law backing) turn down his claim for a deduction, ruling that the increased knowledge he was obtaining was not to enable him to perform his duties but rather to put him in a position to do his duties. The nicety of the distinction means that no tax deduction would be allowed.

The same reasoning applies over your journey to work. While it is of course always necessary to travel to work in order to perform the day's duties it is not possible to claim for the cost of travelling between home and work, as that again simply puts you in a position to do your duties and is not something incurred in the course of actually carrying them out. One might therefore ask what exactly can be claimed, and the answer must be very little, strictly speaking, but the following items are generally allowable:

1. Cost of uniforms and protective clothing including cleaning and replacement. This would not, however, cover such items as suits required by a bank manager in order to present a correct image to his clients.

2. Cost of maintaining and repairing tools, musical instruments and similar items required in the actual performance of a job or profession. This would cover things like micrometers for engineers and plumbing equipment for plumbers.

3. Books and stationery held to be necessary for a job. This might be technical textbooks for university teachers or medical textbooks for doctors.

4. Extra costs incurred when using part of your home as an office. This would only be allowed if working at home were part of your normal duties. Again, this might cover lecturers and teachers who have to do marking or lecture and lesson preparation at home.

5. Travelling costs while performing your duties would be allowable. If you travelled to work in the normal way that part of the travelling costs would not be allowed, but if you then travelled, say, 100 miles to visit a customer and then returned to the office, the 200 miles and the related cost would be regarded as business expenditure. This would be allowed whether the journey was made by car, train or another mode of transport.

6. Hotel and meal expenses are normally allowable when

travelling in the course of your job if you have also maintained a permanent home. Normally you are entitled to subsistence payments for meals taken while out of the office on an extended visit of, say, more than five hours. The Revenue would not, however, allow excessive costs of meals and the type of allowance that they are likely to agree is around £3 to £4 per day.

7. Club subscriptions are normally not allowed even if you are required to take clients to the club for entertainment purposes. If, however, the subscription is to enable you to use club facilities for overnight business stays as an alternative to staying in a hotel, then the cost would be held to be allowable. In trades such as plumbing where it is customary to provide your own tools or clothing, many trade unions have agreed with the Inland Revenue a fixed deduction of, say, £80 per year. This amount may be claimed without proof that the money has actually been spent. If you have spent more, then the Revenue would accept higher amounts if there was proof of payment. You should check with the union concerned to see whether any scheme is in force with the Revenue.

8. It is also possible to claim allowances for the depreciation of a car which you have had to provide personally for use in carrying out the duties of a job. Any allowances given are restricted to take account of private use.

EXPENSES WHICH CANNOT BE CLAIMED
The expense of items which it is felt are needed to do the job properly but which are not necessary because other people could do the job without them are not, in general, allowable.

The initial costs of tools and instruments for which you can claim the cost of replacements are not deductible.

The cost of entertaining customers would also not be allowed, unless the employer concerned reimbursed the cost to the employee.

Prior to 15th March 1988, a business received a deduction for the cost of entertaining or of making a gift to an overseas customer. From the 15th March 1988 these allowances have been withdrawn and overseas customers are now in the same category as UK customers. Though an employee will not be taxed on re-imbursed business expenses his employer will have the cost disallowed in his tax computation.

Any costs incurred on entertaining your own colleagues would not be allowed. This could cover such items as two building society managers lunching together to discuss the latest problems in their areas. If one claimed the cost of entertaining the other this would be disallowed by the Revenue and, if reimbursed by his employer, the employee would be taxed on it as a benefit.

The rental element of your home telephone will never be allowable as a deduction, but it is possible to claim those calls that relate to business. If, therefore, a telephone bill was £200 and £60 of this was for the rental of the lines and the equipment and 50 per cent of the calls were for business purposes, then it would be possible to claim £70 of the cost as an expense against your employment earnings.

Cases which have been through the courts showed that the following claims were not allowable:

- Cost of domestic assistance where the wife was employed.
- The cost of looking after a widower's children.
- Articled clerk's examination fees.
- Employment agency's fees to obtain a position.
- Telephone and other expenses of consultant anaesthetist.
- Flat-rate expenses for employee.

Box 57
It is possible for those in employment to claim fees paid to certain professional bodies and learned societies if the activities are relevant to the job carried out. Those who carry on a trade or a profession will claim the cost directly in their accounts and so should not also enter anything at Box 57. Those in employment may claim whatever the society to which they belong has advised them is deductable for tax purposes. The Revenue have a long list of associations and societies whose costs they accept may be allowable in all or in part against earnings. Once on the list the fees paid to the body concerned will always be allowed as a

deduction but it can be quite difficult to persuade the Revenue to add a new body to the list.

Payments to such bodies as the Institute of Directors are usually allowable for tax purposes.

INTEREST ON LOANS

Interest on loans for the purchase or improvement of property in the UK
Do not include bank overdrafts

Loans for only or main residence

58-60

Building society loan at 5/4/88 *Do not put amounts*

| Name of society | Account number | Please tick box if you did not pay under the net interest arrangements (MIRAS) ▶ ☐ |

Building society loan paid off in year to 5/4/88 *Do not put amounts*

| Name of society | Account number | Please tick box if you did not pay under the net interest arrangements (MIRAS) ▶ ☐ |

All other lenders *Include amounts*

| | | Self | Wife |
| Name(s) of lender(s) | Account number(s) | £ | £ |

If all interest is paid net to a lender other than a Building Society, enclose an interest certificate **only** where you claim tax relief for rates higher than basic rate. Always enclose an interest certificate if you paid any interest outside the MIRAS arrangements.

Box 58

Details should be entered here of monies borrowed for the
purchase or improvement of properties in the United Kingdom or
the Republic of Ireland, but see below for the position on
improvement loans after 6th April 1988. The property must be the
main residence of the claimant and for this purpose a married
couple can only have one main residence. It is possible in certain
circumstances, for instance publicans who are in job-related
accommodation, to claim interest relief on a property in which
for most of their time they do not reside. There have also been
tax cases in which it was held that a weekend property could be a
main residence qualifying for interest relief if that was where the
owners considered their main residence to be and their weekday
home was for job purposes only.

The 1988 Finance Bill abolishes any relief on loans for home
improvements made on or after 6th April 1988. This is so even
though the home improvement loan taken together with another
loan may well only total, say, £20,000. The moral of this is, of
course, that anyone buying a house who intends to add a garage
to it later would be well advised to include the garage at the
outset, since if the total loan is less than £30,000 full interest
relief will then be received.

Relief is limited to the interest on £30,000 per year, but there is no limit to the rate the interest may be. Until 1st August 1988 unmarried borrowers clubbing together to buy a house could each receive the £30,000 interest relief allowing, for instance, three people to have full tax relief on £90,000. The 1988 Finance Bill however proposes that from 1st August 1988 new loan interest relief will be limited to £30,000, irrespective of the number of people borrowing to purchase that residence. This brings people sharing the purchase of a home into line with married couples and ends the situation where there was a tax penalty on marriage. The new rules only apply to loans taken out after 1st August 1988 and any existing loans to sharers continue to enjoy full individual relief. But if two people who are enjoying £60,000 worth of mortgage interest relief sell that property they would be limited to the new limit of just £30,000 on any property they bought in its place.

The Budget proposed that the £30,000 limit can be transferred in circumstances where otherwise unmarried sharers with unequal loans would not be able to use all the limit between them. This new rule is shown by the following example:

'A' has a loan of £25,000
'B' has a loan of £8,000
'C' has a loan of £5,000

Normally this would mean that each would have a ceiling of £10,000 with the effect that 'B' and 'C' would have all their interest relieved but 'A' would have only £10,000 relieved. In such circumstances, therefore, it will be possible for 'B' and 'C' to transfer their unused limits to 'A' so that 'A' will be entitled to relief on a total of £17,000, made up of his own £10,000 figure plus £2,000 from 'B' and £5,000 from 'C'. In this way £30,000 of the total loan of £38,000 qualifies for relief despite the unequal distribution.

Normally interest relief is given under the mortgage interest relief at source system (MIRAS). If you are only taxable at the basic rate then the MIRAS system takes care of all tax relief, but if tax relief is due at a higher rate the adjustment will be given in a tax assessment. If mortgage interest relief is not given at source then all interest paid will be allowed under a Schedule E

assessment and in such circumstances it is necessary to obtain a
certificate of interest paid from the lender.

Both banks and building societies operate the MIRAS system.
You are required to enter on the tax return the name of the
building society and the account number, but if this has been
unchanged for a number of years then an entry 'per previous
year' is sufficient. If the loan is a mixed one, for example £30,000
borrowed to buy a property and £20,000 for another non-
qualifying purpose, such as to buy a yacht, then a note should be
made of this and relief claimed on 30/50ths of the interest paid.
Similarly if part of the interest is for your trade, profession or
vocation, then that part of the interest should be claimed in the
trading accounts and not as a personal deduction.

Box 59
This box should include interest on loans used for the purchase
or improvement of a property, caravan or houseboat of the
taxpayer, or his divorced or separated wife. This is so whether the
residence is owned by the separated or divorced wife or jointly.
Relief is at present due on loans to buy property occupied by a
widowed, divorced or separated mother or mother-in-law or any
other relative who is unable to work because of old age (65 or
over), permanent illness or disablement and who occupies the
residence rent free and without any other form of payment.

The £30,000 mortgage interest relief is spread between each
of these properties, so if you had a £20,000 mortgage on your
own property and a separate £20,000 mortgage on a house for a
dependent relative, then relief would only be given on a total of
one half of the interest on the dependent relative's property.

The 1988 Finance Bill proposes to abolish the dependent
relatives' loan interest relief scheme where loans are offered on or
after 6th April 1988. Relief continues for the life of existing loans
which already qualify under the rules. In future, therefore, it
would be better to arrange matters so that the relative pays the
interest and therefore can enjoy loan interest relief.

A note should be given of the balance outstanding on the last
statement provided by the lender. This will usually be slightly to
the taxpayer's advantage as it will include any amount paid off in

the year so, when the Revenue work out the fraction of what amount of the interest is allowable, if the loan is over £30,000 there will be a slightly higher amount allowed than would be strictly due. It is also a useful tip to pay off if possible a lump sum just ahead of the date at which the building society or bank takes its balance for the year, since that will reduce both the balance and the interest payable in the following year.

BRIDGING LOANS

If you have changed properties during the year, then it is quite usual to have a bridging loan and the Revenue are prepared to give a second £30,000 worth of relief on the bridging loan if certain conditions are fulfilled. These usually cover a straightforward case where you have a £30,000 loan on your old property and buy a new property with a £40,000 loan, replacing the original loan with a £30,000 bridging loan. The interest on this will usually be allowed in addition to three quarters of the loan interest on the new property. The Revenue will generally allow these provisions to cover bridging loans for up to twelve months and will, at their discretion, extend the twelve-month period if it is difficult, for example, to sell the old property, provided it is actively being marketed and is not being used for another purpose in the meantime.

INTEREST ON OVERDRAFTS AND CREDIT CARDS

Under no circumstances is it ever possible to obtain relief for interest paid on overdrafts and credit cards except in the limited circumstances of bank overdraft interest paid relating to a trade, profession or vocation. Even if £30,000 was borrowed on overdraft to buy a house, the interest paid would not be deductible for tax purposes as it was not a loan. Loans which take the place of a previous overdraft are also not always allowable for tax relief purposes so you should always ensure that if interest relief is to be claimed you take out a loan right from the start. A loan which replaces an otherwise qualifying loan is itself qualifying.

Many people employed by banks and building societies receive the benefit of low-interest loans from their employer.

They are not taxable on the benefit of that low-interest loan up to the £30,000 limit because if they had actually paid a normal rate of interest on that loan they would have been entitled to tax relief on it.

Loans above the £30,000 limit are taxed in the normal way of beneficial loans, that is, it is deemed that the taxpayer should have paid a notional interest charge of some $10\frac{1}{2}$ per cent, and the difference between what was actually paid and the $10\frac{1}{2}$ per cent averaged out over the entire loan is taxed as a benefit.

These principles apply not just to houses but also to caravans or houseboats. As long as it is fully equipped as a residence, then interest borrowed to buy such property is allowable just as if it were a normal building on dry land. No loan interest relief would, however, be allowable if a home was purchased in a country other than the United Kingdom or the Republic of Ireland. So if you chose to live in France and have rented accommodation in England during the working week, then the fact that loan interest was being paid on the property in France would not entitle you to a deduction for tax purposes, even though the Revenue might well accept it was your main residence.

Outgoings: 6 April 1987 to 5 April 1988

Interest on loans for the purchase or improvement of property in the UK continued
Do not include bank overdrafts

61	Let property (other than furnished holiday lets)		Number of weeks let	Self	Wife
	Address *enclose certificate*			£	£

Box 61 **LET PROPERTY**
Interest on loans to purchase or improve property in the United Kingdom or the Republic of Ireland which is let or to be let is eligible for tax relief without any limit on the amount of borrowings. The conditions are that in any period of 52 weeks comprising the time when interest is payable the property concerned must be let at a commercial rent for more than 26 weeks, or is either available for letting at a commercial rent or is used as a main residence or the residence of a dependent relative or a former or separated spouse of the taxpayer. Any period

when the house is unavailable because of any construction or repairs can be ignored.

Interest may only be set against the rental income received and if the interest exceeds the rental income then the interest may be relieved against letting of any land, caravan or houseboat in that year. If income for the year of assessment is insufficient, then the excess interest may be carried forward and set off in future years against income from the same property or any other land, caravan or houseboat.

An interest certificate from the lender should again be provided with the tax return.

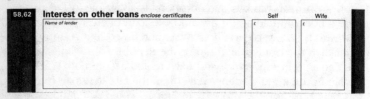

Box 62   *INTEREST ON OTHER LOANS*

It is also possible to obtain interest relief on other loans and Box 62 is the place to make such claims. Again, the name of the lender should be given and the certificate of interest should be shown. There is effectively no limit on the amount of interest which may be claimed so long as the purpose for which it is borrowed is a qualifying one. The type of qualifying purposes covered are as follows:

1. The acquisition of part of the ordinary share capital of a close company (this is generally a company controlled by five or fewer persons), or for lending money to a close company in which the lender either works in a managerial capacity or in which he on his own or with his associates owns more than 5 per cent of the ordinary share capital. Money lent to one's own family company to carry out some trading purposes would mean that full interest relief would be due on the money borrowed.

2. Money used to acquire an interest in a partnership or for lending to a partnership for use in its business also qualifies for interest relief as long as the money stays with the partnership. If it is subsequently withdrawn, then the interest relief is reduced proportionately. It is not possible for a sole trader to lend money to his business and his only method of obtaining tax relief is for his business to claim tax relief in the accounts themselves. The personal advantage in obtaining tax relief in the year when the interest is paid rather than on a previous year basis of assessment is, therefore, available only to those lending money to a close company or a partnership.

3. Money borrowed to purchase plant or machinery used by a partnership or used within your own employment can also qualify for relief, but you are not eligible for relief on interest falling due and payable more than three years after the end of the year of assessment in which the debt was incurred.

4. Loans secured on your only or main residence and used to purchase a life annuity are also eligible for interest relief if certain restrictions are met. These are that not less than $\frac{9}{10}$ of the proceeds of the loan are applied to the purchase of an annuity ending with the life of the purchaser or with the life of the survivor of two or more persons, including the person to whom the loan was made. Also at the time the loan was made each annuitant must have attained the age of 65, and the final condition is that the loan was secured on land in the United Kingdom or the Republic of Ireland, and the person to whom it was made, or one of the annuitants, owned an estate or interest in that land and used it as their only or main residence at the time the interest was paid.

5. Tax relief is available on loans to pay Inheritance Tax. Interest relief is only due in respect of a period ending within one year of making the loan.

In general terms, to obtain tax relief you must use the money for one of the purposes within a reasonable time before or after taking out the loan. The Revenue will normally accept that a six month period is a reasonable time so that it is possible to choose which of the qualifying purposes has followed or preceded a loan. It is not, therefore, necessary physically to take a particular loan and apply it for a defined purpose, but merely to expend money on one of the qualifying purposes. It is usually also necessary that you qualify under one of the conditions at the time the interest is paid and not merely at the time that the loan is taken out. If you borrow money to lend to a trading company and that company ceases to trade, then you would not obtain any relief for interest payments made after the date when the company ceased to be a trading, and thus a qualifying, company.

The other forms of interest payment which qualify concern commercial investment properties, for example industrial buildings, on which money has been borrowed. The relief can be given for such borrowings in the same way as for ordinary residential lettings. As long as the property has been let for 26 weeks or more in the year, then interest relief can be given against the rental income. If a property has been let for only, say, 25 weeks of the year then no interest relief will be due against the rental income from that property. It is therefore possible to fall into a tax trap, for while in commercial terms a loss has been made because the total amount paid out, including interest, is greater than the rental income, there would be a profit for Income Tax purposes since the rental income from the 25-week period less any normal outgoings would be taxable.

· 10 ·
OTHER OUTGOINGS

63,66 67	**Other outgoings** *enter gross amounts before deduction of tax* Covenants, bonds of annuity, settlements, covenanted payments to charities, accrued income purchased etc.		Self	Wife
	Details		£	£
64	Alimony, aliment or maintenance paid	*Details*	£	£
65	UK property rents or yearly interest paid to persons abroad	*Details*	£	£
68	**Changes in untaxed income or outgoings since 5 April 1987**	*Details*		

Box 63 PAYMENTS UNDER DEEDS OF COVENANT, BONDS OF ANNUITY

There are two basic categories of covenant, the non-charitable covenant and the charitable convenant. These two categories have different taxation consequences.

1. Non-charitable covenants Covenants made on or after the 15th March 1988 have been taken out of the tax system altogether. The payers do not get tax relief and the recipients will not have to pay tax on the money they have received. People who already have covenants will continue to receive tax relief for as long as the covenant lasts. The following paragraphs therefore describe the pre-15th March 1988 rules. Covenants made before 15th March 1988 must be submitted to the tax office by 30th June 1988 if the taxpayer hopes to continue to benefit under the old rules.

2. Pre-15th March 1988 non-charitable covenants
Tax relief on these covenants was only at the basic rate, so that if you were making a convenant to a student child to pay them £500 per year in a year when the basic rate of tax was 27 per cent, then you would actually only hand over to them £365 in money. They would be able to reclaim from the Revenue the balance of £135, which would have been the tax deducted when making the covenant, if they themselves were not liable to tax because, for example, they could set personal allowances against

the convenant income. The Revenue accepted that covenant payments to students were effective for tax purposes and actually provided an information pack called 'IR59'. This pack described all that was required to set up an effective tax covenant and indicated how the student should claim back the tax deducted at source.

Covenants must have had strict conditions if they were to qualify for tax relief. Non-charitable covenants had for example to be capable of lasting for more than six years, though it was not necessary that they did. A common phraseology used was that 'the payment would be made for seven years or such lesser period of full time education which the student might undertake.' If, therefore, the child was at university for only three years then the covenant itself was only paid for three years. If the child went on to study for a further degree then the covenant would be payable for a much longer period.

It is also important to note that the Revenue expect payments to be made in accordance with the terms of the covenant so that payments should be made at the times specified and not ahead of those dates. Ideally, a standing order should be set up into the child's bank account to keep exactly in line with the terms of the covenant.

There must also be no reciprocation under a covenant if it is to be effective so that you are not in some way receiving any personal benefit for the money expended. It is noted above that covenants were only effective for children over eighteen, but this is not the case if the child involved is somebody else's. It might seem therefore a relatively simple arrangement for two friends to arrange to covenant to each other's child, but there would in this case be reciprocation, so the Revenue would disallow all tax benefits and would look with grave disapproval at any such reciprocal arrangements which were hidden from them.

Ordinary covenants did, however, work and as indicated the typical recipients were either your own children while at university, your grandchildren or nieces, or indeed any friend's children to whom you wished to give money. The generations could of course be reversed and you could make a covenant to your widowed mother if she was at that time not liable to pay

Income Tax. As there was only covenant relief at the basic rate there was absolutely no tax advantage in making the covenant to someone who paid tax in full at the basic rate. It should also be noted that if you made covenant payments while you yourself were not fully or only partly liable to tax then the Revenue could ask you as donor to hand over the basic rate tax you were required to have deducted at source. In the example above, therefore, the £135 could be assessed directly on you as donor if you have not paid at least £135 tax in the ordinary course of events from your income.

3. Charitable covenants These are not affected by the extensive changes to the covenant rules. Covenants to charities must be capable of lasting for more than three years to qualify for relief. There is no limit currently on the amount of the payment to a charity on which you can claim tax relief. As well as the shorter period over which the covenant must be capable of lasting, the Revenue grant higher-rate tax relief on covenants to charity so that if you were liable at a 60 per cent tax rate and covenanted to give a charity £1,000, then you would effectively bear only £400 of the full £1,000. However, you only deduct basic rate tax at source when making the payment to the charity and receive the balance of the tax relief in your tax assessment.

You should enter on the tax return details of the deed and to whom it is payable, together with the gross amount before deduction of tax. In making the payment the donor gives to the donee a certificate that 'x' amount has been deducted at source on a form R185. This form is available from the Revenue and stocks should be obtained if regular covenant payments are made. The R185 certificate may then be used by the charity or indeed the child in order to reclaim any tax involved. The charitable covenant should be shown separately from any non-charitable covenants in order that the Revenue may recognise that higher-rate tax relief is due.

Box 64 **PAYMENTS OF ALIMONY OR MAINTENANCE**

Payments should be entered here which have to be made under a court order, decree of the court, or legally binding agreement for the maintenance of children or a wife from whom there is a legal separation or divorce. It is the gross amount before deduction of tax which is shown on the tax return which would therefore be the gross payment actually made. You should not show voluntary payments for which there is no tax relief, although it may be possible for someone to continue claiming married man's allowance in such circumstances. The Revenue should be provided with a copy of the court order.

Payments under court orders are made without deduction of tax if they are the 'small maintenance payments', referred to at Box 51 on pages 71–72. These are liable to higher-rate tax relief and are therefore a very useful form of tax planning if you have had to go through the unfortunate circumstances of divorce. It is sometimes said, not without a large element of truth, that the only people who can afford private school fees are the wealthy and the divorced. This is because payments in a divorce settlement may be made either to the mother or to the children. If made to the mother they will rank as her income, and if she has any other income they will be taxable to at least the basic rate. If, however, payments are made to the children, then they are initially set against the child's personal allowances and therefore at 1987/88 rates up to £2,425 may be payable with full tax relief to the paying father.

Take the case of a married man with three children who might be paying out £2,000 per annum school fees for each child. On the assumption that before April 5th 1988 he was a 60 per cent taxpayer, in order to pay that £6,000 he would have to earn a gross sum of £15,000. In the divorce situation a mere £6,000 is required to pay the same school fees and there would be no tax paid by the children, as it would be within their personal allowances. This therefore represents a considerable decrease in the family unit's tax contribution to the Revenue. Caution must always be taken in drawing up court orders and in the writer's experience solicitors, while no doubt settling things correctly from the legal point of view, often make serious mistakes from the taxation point of view.

The Revenue have provided sample wording for court orders which will be effective for payment of school fees and these should be strictly followed. It is important that the father should cease all contracts he might have had with the school and that any new contracts should either be entered into by the child or by some agent for the child. The Revenue do not object to the payments being made to the Bursar of a school. If the arrangements before and after divorce are left unchanged so that the school still considers the father to be the one liable to make the payments, then whatever the court order says there will be no tax relief given. This point was in fact tested before the Special Commissioners on behalf of a client by the writer who, being a solicitor, had drawn up his own court order documents, and some £12,000 tax relief was lost through ineffective drafting. A sample of the acceptable draft is shown as an Appendix to this chapter.

Alimony payments are different in that tax is deducted at source by the payer. This is because the amounts payable are outside the small maintenance payment limits. Payments being made to a child would need to be at least £208 per month before exceeding the small maintenance limits. If, however, £400 per month is being paid, then you would deduct basic rate tax at source and at the old rate of 27 per cent you would actually hand over £292 to the recipient. The £108 tax deducted at source would be one part of the tax relief for the payer and any balance of tax relief would be compensated by insertion of an allowance in the tax assessment, which would no doubt be raised. Effectively alimony payments are very similar to deeds of covenant payments to a charity in that you receive full tax relief up to the highest rate. If not liable to tax or only liable in part, the recipient would be able to claim back part or all of the £108 tax deducted at source.

It is not always apparent what the Revenue accepts as being a legal separation. Tax relief on payments to children will only be achievable under a court order. However, it is possible to have a legally binding agreement for payments to a wife without it being a formal court order. As long as there is an agreement which is legally binding so that the wife could if necessary sue the husband for the payments which are due, then this will be regarded as a transfer of income from husband to wife and there

MANAGING YOUR PERSONAL TAXES

will be tax relief for the payments made. From the date of separation the woman is treated as a single person and this can be from a date while the parties are still living in the same house, so long as they are, effectively, separated and carrying on separate existences. The Revenue ask very probing questions on this point, such as whether the couple have separate laundry, eating and social arrangements within the property. If the Revenue can be satisfied they will accept that the parties have separated even though circumstances have forced them to share the same dwelling.

As well as Income Tax allowances for the wife this can have Capital Gains Tax advantages for them and provides scope for tax allowance of any payments made from husband to wife under such an arrangement.

This is just a brief summary of a complicated area and it is mentioned simply to show that it was not absolutely necessary that there be a court order before you could get tax relief or be treated as separated. The reason the Revenue claws back any payments made to children under a legally binding agreement which falls short of a court order is that such payments are treated as remaining the payer's income for tax purposes.

Position after 15th March 1988
The position varies depending on whether the court order in question was taken out before or after 15th March 1988.

Pre-15th March 1988 orders
Payments under these orders including variations to existing orders will continue to be treated under the rules described above for the 1988/89 tax year. Any ex-wife or separated wife receiving payments will, however, not be taxed on the first £1,490 received in 1988/89. Thus if the ex-wife has an order to her of £2,490 she will only be taxed on £1,000 in 1988/89. The payer receives full tax relief as previously on the £2,490 paid in 1988/89. For 1989/90 the taxpayer will only gain tax relief on payments up to the level he received in 1988/89. In arriving at the limit for 1988/89, account will be taken of any payments due in that year and any amending court order or agreements before 6th April

1989. The recipient, however, will be taxable subject to the overriding limit of the amount which was taxable in 1988/89. All payments for maintenance due after 5th April 1989 will be paid gross without tax being deducted by the payer.

New court orders

The recipient of such new orders is not taxable upon the amount received and the payer has relief limited to £1,490 for the 1988/89 period whatever amounts may actually be paid under the court order. Maintenance payments made to children do not qualify for any relief on these post-15th March 1988 orders.

When a person is paying maintenance to more than one divorced or separated spouse, all the payments will count towards the £1,490 for relief purposes.

FOREIGN DIVORCES

If the divorce is effected by a foreign court then the rules indicated above do not necessarily apply. No tax will be deductible from the payments by the United Kingdom resident, but a recipient of alimony from someone abroad will be taxed on receipt.

Box 65 RENTS OR YEARLY INTEREST PAID TO PERSONS LIVING ABROAD

Rent

If someone in the United Kingdom pays rent to an overseas landlord, then he must deduct basic rate tax from each rental payment made. If he fails to do so he can be liable to the United Kingdom Revenue for the amount. While the Taxes Act gives the tenant scope for relief against the landlord for the amounts that the Revenue might ask for, that is often of little practical use if the recipient is abroad and you are no longer paying him·rent. Accordingly therefore anyone who is paying rent to an overseas landlord or, to be more exact, where payment is made (whether in the United Kingdom or elsewhere) directly to a person whose usual place of abode is outside the United Kingdom, must give careful consideration to the taxation position. Advice is that tax should always be deducted at source. It is only if you are paying to an agent, such as an estate agent in the United Kingdom on behalf of an overseas landlord, that you are safe from deducting tax from the rental payment, since in that instance the landlord's agent is required to account to the Revenue for the tax due.

The expression 'usual place of abode' must be carefully watched because it might well be that someone lives in this country for a part of the year but habitually resides outside the United Kingdom. Payment of rent to them in such circumstances would still come within the provisions indicated so that tax would have to be deducted at source.

Interest payments

Within the United Kingdom one individual may pay interest to another without deducting tax at source, though companies must deduct basic rate tax when they make interest payments to individuals or to other companies. However, if annual interest payments are made to someone outside the United Kingdom then, whoever the payer is, he must deduct tax at source.

The term 'annual interest' is complicated to explain but in essence means that the loan agreement is capable of lasting more than one year. If therefore you simply borrowed the money from someone for a two- to three-month period and paid them interest that wouldn't be annual interest and there would be no requirement to deduct tax. You cannot, however, dress up a longer agreement by having a run of six-monthly agreements culminating in a total period of two years and then argue that no interest needs to be deducted at source. In such circumstances the Revenue would argue that this was a sham and that you had entered into a two-year agreement for which the interest was annual and therefore tax had to be deducted.

It is sometimes possible to alter the situation so that the payment of interest is not to an overseas resident but rather to a United Kingdom bank. The overseas resident might have deposited an equivalent amount with an overseas branch of the same bank so that the bank had no risk upon its funds and simply took a small percentage fee for entering into the transaction. In such circumstances there is no need to deduct tax from source and the arrangement is known as 'back-to-back financing'. While the Revenue do not always challenge such arrangements it should be noted that unless each step of the transaction stands up commercially when looked at in isolation, they might regard the arrangement as a sham and declare that tax should be deducted at source from the interest payment.

The entry to go on the tax return is the name of the person to whom the money was paid, an abbreviated address and the amount of rent or interest.

The overseas landlord will not necessarily suffer as much tax on the gross rent as this basic rate deduction represents. He is entitled to put in accounts to the Revenue so that if he is paying interest in order to buy the United Kingdom property and his interest and other expenses are substantial, then the tax on the rent deducted at source would usually be returned to him.

A tax tip on this point for any overseas resident who lets property in the United Kingdom is that any money they borrow to buy UK property should always be borrowed from a UK bank with the interest on the loan being payable in the United Kingdom. This should ensure tax relief on it.

Box 66 PAYMENTS UNDER THE IRISH CHURCH AND LANDS ACTS

No one has ever been seen to make an entry in this somewhat obscure spot on the return. But the section is there and if, by chance, the reader has paid any amount of tithe rent charge or land annuity under these provisions an entry should be made on the return, since a proportion of the payments is allowable as a deduction for tax purposes.

Box 67 ACCRUED INCOME

In the 1987 Finance Act the Revenue brought in anti-avoidance provisions which stopped people, often those who were higher-rate taxpayers, from selling securities cum-dividend just before sale and thus getting a higher price for them than they would otherwise have done. This effectively meant that instead of paying Income Tax on the interest or dividend received they would only pay Capital Gains Tax at a maximum of 30 per cent on the higher price received for the security. The Revenue have introduced some elaborate legislation to stop this practice and this in effect ensures that anyone who has more than £5,000 worth of these securities is affected.

Under the accrued income provisions, interest on securities is treated as accruing on a day-to-day basis between interest payment days. When the securities are transferred after 27th February 1986 a person is charged Income Tax on the income that accrued before the final interest period of his ownership, with appropriate adjustment to his income and also to the transferee. So if someone has received something cum-dividend part of the accrued income might be deducted from the interest he would otherwise be chargeable upon in the relevant tax year. The position is very complicated but there is a Revenue pamphlet IR68 available describing in brief terms the basic rules of the accrued income scheme. These provisions are of no interest to those whose holdings do not exceed £5,000.

Box 68   CHANGES IN UNTAXED INCOME OR OUTGOINGS SINCE 5th APRIL 1987

The taxpayer should give details here, including relevant dates and amounts, of any alterations since the previous year in sources of income not taxed before receipt. For example, if someone has won £500,000 on the football pools this might be an appropriate place to mention it so that the Revenue do not become suspicious about increased deposits in the building society, which are reflected in the tax return. Equally, any legacies which have been received in the year should be entered at this part of the tax return, as that again can explain any sudden and otherwise inexplicable increases of capital.

Any accounts which have been closed in the year should also be mentioned at this point, indicating the date that the account was closed. Few, if any, questions are usually raised upon the information put in this particular box of the return.

Appendix to Box 64   PRACTICE DIRECTION (MINOR: PAYMENT OF SCHOOL FEES)

Maintenance orders which contain an element in respect of

school fees frequently have to be varied when the school fees increase. This requirement could be avoided if the relevant part of the maintenance order were to be automatically adjusted when the school fees go up.

The Inland Revenue have agreed to this principle. A form of order which they found acceptable is as follows:

> 'It is ordered that the (petitioner) (respondent) do pay or cause to be paid to the child AB as from the day of
> 19   until (he) (she) shall attain the age of 17 years (or for so long as (he) (she) shall continue to receive full-time education) or further order periodical payments for (himself) (herself)
> (a) of an amount equivalent to such sum as after deduction of income tax at the basic rate equals the school fees (but not the extras in the school bill) (including specified extras) at the school the said child attends for each financial year (by way of three payments on   ) (payable monthly); together with
> (b) the sum of £   per annum less tax payable monthly in respect of general maintenance of the said child.'

It should be noted that, even if the amount referred to in part (b) is within the current limits of small maintenance payments, it should still be expressed as 'less tax' because the relevant figure for the maintenance order will be the combined total of the two parts.

In such cases the Revenue will require to be satisfied that the payer under the order has no contractual liability for payment of the school fees.

If an order expressed as payable to the child, whether made in this form, or in a form which includes an element in respect of school fees for a specific amount, also provides that payment of the school fees should be made direct to the school (because, for example, it is feared that the other spouse might dissipate it) the Revenue have agreed subject to the condition hereafter set out, that tax relief will be given on that element. The wording of the order should be

'And it is further ordered that that part of the order which reflects the school fees shall be paid to the (Headmaster) (Bursar) (School Secretary) as agent for the said child and the receipt of that payee shall be sufficient discharge.'

The school fees should be paid *in full* and should be paid out of the net amount under the maintenance order after deduction of tax. Certificates for the full tax deduction should continue to be provided by the other spouse (or other person referred to in rule 69 of the Matrimonial Causes Rules 1977, S.I. 1977, No. 344) in the normal way.

A form of contract which is acceptable to the Inland Revenue is as follows:

'THIS AGREEMENT is made between THE GOVERNORS OF
. . . .
by their duly authorised officer   . . . .
(hereinafter called "the school") of the first part: . . . .
. . . .
and the (Headmaster) (Bursar) (School Secretary) of the
second part, and . . . .
(hereinafter called "the Child") of the third part.

WHEREAS (it is proposed to ask the   . . . .
Court to make an order) (the   . . . .
Court has made an order) in cause number   . . . .
that the Father of the Child do make periodical payments to the child at the rate of £ . . . . per annum less tax until the Child completes full-time education (or as the case may be) and that that part of the order which reflects the school fees shall be paid to the (Headmaster) (Bursar) (School Secretary) as agent for the Child and the receipt of that agent shall be a sufficient discharge.

1. The Child hereby constitutes the (Headmaster) (Bursar) (School Secretary) to be his agent for the purpose of receiving the said fees and the Child agrees to pay the said fees to the said School in consideration of being educated there.

2. In consideration of the said covenant the (Headmaster) (Bursar) (School Secretary) agrees to accept the said payments by the Father as payments on behalf of the Child and the School agrees to educate the Child during such time as the said school fees are paid.

Dated the   day of   19   .'

This direction supersedes the registrar's direction of 10th November 1980, which is hereby cancelled: See *Practice Direction (Minor: School Fees) (1980)* 1 WLR 1441.
Issued with the concurrence of the Lord Chancellor.

The wording of the court order above is useful in checking whether your existing court orders are in the correct wording in order to obtain relief. It must be appreciated, however, that following the 1988 Finance Bill becoming law, no future court orders in the form shown would be effective for tax purposes since orders to children are outside the tax system.

· 11 ·
CAPITAL GAINS

The 1988 Budget was foreshadowed in the pre-Budget publicity as the Act in which Capital Gains Tax might be abolished. Mr Lawson did not take quite such a radical step but did completely alter the basis on which capital gains were taxed. He made two major changes of principle. These apply to disposals on or after 6th April 1988.

1. *BASE PERIOD* The value of all assets liable to Capital Gains Tax are rebased to 1982 if they were owned before that date. Instead of using the acquisition cost in any Capital Gains Tax disposal one now uses the 31st March 1982 value. This removes all liability on inflationary capital gains which may have built up in the 1970s. Since indexation relief (see page 107) is also based on the 31st March 1982 value, Capital Gains Tax now only arises on increases in value over and above the inflation indexed value of the asset at 31st March 1982.

There are provisions to ensure that the 1982 rebasing does not increase the amount of a gain or loss compared with what it would have been under the previous regime. If an asset is worth less at 31st March 1982 than its cost then it will be possible to use the cost figure and so reduce the gain that would otherwise have arisen. Also if an asset is sold at a loss and that loss is greater under the new system because the 31st March 1982 value was higher than the cost, the allowable loss will be calculated against cost rather than the 31st March 1982 value. If using a 31st March 1982 value there is a loss when an asset is sold but reference to cost under the old system would have shown a gain, then the transaction will be treated as one on which there is neither a gain nor a loss arising.

2. *THE RATE OF CAPITAL GAINS TAX* The rate of Capital Gains Tax has stayed unchanged at 30 per cent for individuals since its inception in April 1965. This has been changed by the 1988 Finance Bill in that the rate of tax will be the same as the marginal rate of Income Tax for the person making the gain. This means that the rate of tax could be anything between nil and 40 per cent. The way in which this works is illustrated by the following example:

Example 1 An individual has taxable income for 1988/89 (after reliefs and allowances) of £12,000 and capital gains above the annual exemption limit of £4,000. When treated as the top slice of income the gains of £4,000 plus income do not exceed the basic rate limit of £19,300. Accordingly the gains will be chargeable to Capital Gains Tax at a rate equivalent to the basic rate of Income Tax of 25 per cent in 1988/9.

Example 2 An individual has taxable income for 1988/89 (after reliefs and allowances) of £15,000 and gains above the annual exemption of £11,000. When treated as the top slice of income, the gains of £11,000 result in the basic rate limit of £19,300 being exceeded. Accordingly gains of £4,300 will be chargeable to Capital Gains Tax at a rate equivalent to the basic rate of Income Tax (25 per cent in 1988/89), and gains of £6,700 at a rate equivalent to the higher rate of Income Tax (40 per cent in 1988/89).

The changes affect gains for the tax year 1988/89. The entries on the 1988/89 tax return illustrated in this book cover the year up to 5th April 1988 which are under the old system and therefore details are given below on how to compute capital gains under the old system. Reference to the changes proposed in the 1988 Finance Bill are given where relevant.

Capital Gains: 6 April 1987 to 5 April 1988			
70-80	**Chargeable assets disposed of**	*Amount of gain for year*	
	Date of disposal Description	Self	Wife
		£	£

Box 70
You should enter here what chargeable assets have been disposed of in the year, giving both the date of disposal and the

description of the assets which have been sold. You should then also show the amount of the gain for the year, showing in a separate schedule how this was arrived at if the position is complicated, which it always would be if more than one asset has been sold. The Revenue provide an excellent booklet on Capital Gains Tax headed CGT 8, which should certainly be obtained by anyone who frequently makes gains.

Capital Gains Tax arises on the sale of the majority of assets and includes deals in any form of property and money other than sterling. It is quite possible to buy a large amount of American dollars and sell them at some other time of the year, in which case the gain (or loss) arising would be chargeable (or allowable) for Capital Gains Tax. If you had used the American dollars to buy an asset there would be two disposals to consider, first the asset itself where you would translate acquisition and disposal prices into pounds sterling in order to calculate whether a gain or loss had been made, and secondly the currency involved if that had been held for a substantial period either side of the transaction.

A disposal includes the sale, exchange or gift of an asset (although it is possible to hold over the gain on the gift of an asset if the recipient is an individual or trust resident in the United Kingdom). If someone owned a United Kingdom property which had cost him £10,000 and was now worth £60,000, then a gift to a relative living in America would result in a capital gain of £50,000 before any other reliefs had been accounted for, and tax would be due from the donor, even though they received no financial benefit from the transaction.

If a capital loss arises from a disposal then relief is allowable against any other gains of the year. If, after setting the losses which arise against other capital gains of the same year, there is still a loss it can be carried forward without limit on the period until there is a gain against which it can be set.

A capital loss is computed in exactly the same way as a capital gain would be. It can only be set against other gains and cannot be carried back against the capital gains of a previous year. It is also generally not possible to set capital losses against the taxpayer's income.

The one exception to this rule is the losses which arise on the disposal of shares by an individual who subscribed for shares in a qualifying trading company. The major qualifications are that the company must be a trading company on the date of disposal or have ceased to be a trading company at a time not more than three years before that date and must not have been turned into an investment company. In addition, the company must not have had any of its shares quoted on a recognised stock exchange.

This tax relief provides a valuable support for someone who might wish to invest in a friend's trading company so that if everything went disastrously wrong he does at least get relief against other income. If the relevant election is not made then, as normal, the capital loss arising on such shares is either set against other gains of the year or carried forward.

It is often advantageous to 'bed and breakfast' shares before the 5th April if you have made gains on other shares in the period. If, for example, someone had made £15,000 worth of gains in a year and had some other shares which were standing at a £5,000 loss, it would be possible to sell the shares and repurchase them, thus crystalising the £5,000 loss which could be set against the capital gain, reducing the total amount to £10,000. Be careful, however, not to overdo the situation, since if the gains arising were only £7,000 and you reduced that by the £5,000 loss through a 'bed and breakfast' transaction, you would be wasting the annual Capital Gains Tax exemption referred to below (see pages 112–113).

Not all assets are relevant for Capital Gains Tax and a list of the assets which are exempt is given below (see Box 72, pages 113–115).

While the Revenue will always agree (or otherwise) a Capital Gains Tax computation for a year they will not necessarily comment on a capital loss, since in their view this is only effective when there is a capital gain to relieve it against. The taxpayer concerned should always keep his own list of capital losses, since it may be many years before they are any use to him and he should not rely on the Revenue remembering which years he has shown a capital loss on his tax return. It is very difficult if you have made a capital loss in the mid-1970s of, say, £10,000 to remember in 1988 when you at long last make a capital gain that this valuable relief is still available to you.

Working out your capital gain is sometimes a complicated procedure, as it depends if the asset was held before the inception of Capital Gains Tax in April 1965 or prior to 31st March 1982, which is the relevant date for an indexation relief election (see page 111). Here are three examples to illustrate the computation of gain/loss that should be inserted on the tax return. The rules shown are only applicable to pre-6th April 1988 disposals.

EXAMPLE 1: POST 31st MARCH 1982 ACQUISITION

Let us assume that on 1st January 1983 Mr X bought a property costing £10,000, which he used for rental purposes and never lived in himself. He then sells that property on 1st November 1987 for £70,000. His gain is £60,000, from which he is entitled to deduct all the usual costs of sale, solicitor's, estate agent's and valuation fees. He is not allowed to deduct the cost of repair and decoration of the property throughout the years or revenue items such as rates or mortgage interest. Taking this gross gain therefore of £60,000 there are then two further reliefs available, assuming this is his only disposal in the year. The first is indexation relief, which is calculated on the rise in the retail price

	1982	1983	1984	1985	1986	1987	1988
January	–	82.61	86.84	91.20	96.25	100.0	103.3
February	–	82.97	87.20	91.99	96.60	100.4	103.7
March	79.44	83.12	87.48	92.80	96.73	100.6	
April	81.04	84.28	88.64	94.78	97.67	101.8	
May	81.62	84.64	88.97	95.21	97.85	101.9	
June	81.85	84.84	89.20	95.41	97.79	101.9	
July	81.88	85.30	89.10	95.18	97.52	101.8	
August	81.90	85.68	89.94	95.49	97.82	102.1	
September	81.85	86.06	90.11	95.44	98.30	102.4	
October	82.26	86.36	90.67	95.59	98.45	102.9	
November	82.66	86.67	90.95	95.92	99.29	103.4	
December	82.51	86.89	90.87	96.05	99.62	103.3	

index over the four-year period of ownership. The relevant table is shown below left, from which the increases in the retail prices index can be seen.

RETAIL PRICES INDEX (RPI) TABLE

Gains arising on the disposal of an asset may be reduced by an indexation allowance. This is calculated from increases in the retail prices index taking place after March 1982. The index was re-referenced in January 1987 from 394.5 to 100. The following figures have been worked back from the new base and are not those produced at the time by the Department of Employment.

Indexation relief calculation

Retail prices index 1st January 1983			=	82.61
Retail prices index 1st November 1987			=	103.4
Increase	=	$103.4 \div 82.61 - 1$	=	0.252

The indexation relief available is therefore

£10,000 × 0.252	=	£2,520

Assuming that the £10,000 purchase price includes all incidental costs of buying the property and the £70,000 sale proceeds is the amount received net of all legal and other expenses, the full Capital Gains Tax computation will be as follows:

Capital gains computation

Sale price (net)	£70,000
Purchase cost (gross)	£10,000
Gross gain	£60,000
Indexation relief	£2,520
Annual exemption 1987/88	£6,600
Net chargeable gain	£50,880
Tax @ 30% =	£15,264

EXAMPLE 2: PROPERTY ACQUIRED AFTER APRIL 1965 BUT BEFORE MARCH 1982.

There are now two calculations to do since the taxpayer has the option of electing that the indexation relief which will be based upon the increase in the retail prices index between March 1982 and the date of sale should be a proportion not necessarily of cost but perhaps rather of the value of the asset in March 1982. Assuming the same figures as in the previous example, but including the additional factor that the property was bought in 1980 and was worth £20,000 in 1982, the two computations will be as follows:

Using cost

Sale	£70,000
Purchase	£10,000
Gross gain	£60,000
Indexation relief	£3,020
(increase in RPI from March 1982 to November 1987)	
Less annual exemption	£6,600
Chargeable net gain	£50,380
Tax arising	£15,114

Using March 1982 valuation

Sale	£70,000
Purchase	£10,000
Indexation relief	£6,040
(based upon the March 1982 value of £20,000 and the increase in the RPI index from March 1982 to November 1987)	
Annual exemption	£6,600
Net chargeable gain	£47,360
Tax arising	£14,208

It is clear that in this case it is better to elect using the March 1982 value rather than the actual cost. This will always be the case if the asset has increased in value between the date of purchase and March 1982. If the reverse was the position, it would be better to use cost rather than March 1982 as the basis for indexation relief.

EXAMPLE 3: PRE-APRIL 1965 PURCHASES
If the assets involved are quoted shares then the base cost of the Capital Gains Tax computation is not the actual cost of the asset but rather the value of those shares on the stock market in April 1965. The balance of the capital gain computation follows the normal lines.

If, however, the assets involved are unquoted shares or land without development land value, then it is possible either to use the cost in the computation and to take out of the taxable profit the element of gain which applies when spread over the years to the pre-April 1965 period of ownership, or to elect for the April 1965 value and use that instead of the time-apportioned gain. The result of this potential election is shown in the example below.

It is assumed here that the figures are as above but that the cost was now in April 1960 and that the asset had a value in March 1982 of £40,000 before it was sold for £70,000. Therefore it is bound to be beneficial to elect for the March 1982 basis for indexation relief, and it only remains to calculate whether time

---

Using time-apportionment basis

The Capital Gains Tax computation will be as follows:

Sale price	£70,000
Cost	£10,000
Gross gain	£60,000
Indexation relief	£12,080
	(Based on March 1982 value of £40,000)
Net gain	£47,920

apportionment should be used or the April 1965 value. This is taken as being £16,000.

Using April 1965 valuation

The Capital Gains Tax computation will be as follows:

Sale price £70,000

Deemed purchase cost £16,000

(*Value in April 1965*)

Gross gain £54,000

Less indexation relief £12,080

(*as above*)

Net gain £41,920

The chargeable gain arising is calculated on the $22 \frac{7}{12}$ of the period of ownership arising after April 1965 compared to the total period of ownership of $27 \frac{7}{12}$. This fraction is 0.8187, and when multiplied against the gain indicated above gives a total chargeable gain before annual exemption of £39,232.
It is thus apparent in this case that the April 1965 valuation is not beneficial as the time-apportionment method gives a lower chargeable gain. No April 1965 valuation election would therefore be considered relevant.

The above examples have shown sales of property but often, of course, capital gains arise from share dealing rather than property. Shares are treated in a different way for tax purposes in that holdings of the same share are pooled, so that when a sale is made the share sold is not identified with other shares bought but rather with the whole holding of that share that the taxpayer possesses. To complicate matters even further the taxpayer is considered to have more than one pool of shares, depending on when he acquired them. They are divided into three pools, the first being securities acquired on or after the March 1982 date, the second being the 1982 holding which applies to all shares held at the March 1982 date, and the third refers to those held on 6th April 1985 which had not previously been pooled.

The rules are that securities disposed of are identified (in order of priority) as:

- Securities acquired on or after the 1982 date.
- Securities forming part of a 1982 holding.
- Other securities on a last in first out basis.

There are special rules for disposals on or before the date of acquisition, or acquisitions and disposals within a ten-day period. In general, however, securities are largely identified as those acquired on a last in, first out basis. This has the advantage of minimising the capital gain which arises when looking at the cost of your share portfolio.

SEPARATE ASSESSMENT OF CAPITAL GAINS

A married couple may choose to have their capital gains treated separately so that a wife's losses would not be set against a husband's gains, and so perhaps wasting the capital gains exemption for the year. The Revenue must be told before 6th July of the tax year following that in which the loss or gain arises if this election is to be effective.

INDEPENDENT TAXATION

For 1988/89 and 1989/90 the gains of the wife will continue to be assessed on the husband. This means that the couple's aggregate gains will be taxed (broadly as with investment income) at the rates that would apply if they were the marginal slice of the husband's income, and they will share one annual exemption.

From 6th April 1990 it is proposed that married couples should be taxed independently on their capital gains with separate annual exemptions and so remove yet another of the tax penalties arising on marriage. The provision which allows the losses of one partner to be set against the gains of the other will be abolished.

There will be no change in the rule under which transfers of assets between husband and wife are exempt. It will, therefore, be possible to transfer assets between husband and wife before disposal to ensure that the rate of tax payable is at the lowest possible level, depending on their comparative incomes. A reasonable further period of ownership by the transferee should be allowed to forestall any suggestion by the Revenue of tax avoidance.

Box 71 *ANNUAL EXEMPTION*

The annual exemption for the years up to 1987/88 is relatively generous. In view of the radical reform to Capital Gains Tax from 6th April 1988 the annual exemption for 1988/89 is actually lower than for 1987/88. This means that anyone making short-term gains on assets acquired since 6th April 1982 would pay more Capital Gains Tax under the new regime than under the old rules.

Until 6th April 1990 only one annual exemption per person or married couple is allowed. The annual exemptions for the current and past years are shown below.

In 1987/88 where the total chargeable gains before losses do not exceed £6,600 and the total disposal proceeds of all disposals do not exceed £13,200 it is sufficient to enter in the appropriate section of the tax return the words 'Gains not exceeding £6,600 and disposal proceeds not exceeding £13,200.' Where husband and wife are living together this requirement relates to the combined gains and disposal proceeds of both, but where husbands and wives have applied to be treated separately the gains can be shown on individual returns.

The annual exempt amounts are:

1988/89	£5,000
1987/88	£6,600
1986/87	£6,300
1985/86	£5,900
1984/85	£5,600
1983/84	£5,300
1982/83	£5,000

Only individuals are entitled to these amounts; companies have no exempt amounts and trusts have an exempt allowance of half this amount. Children, however, are entitled to exactly the same allowances as parents and therefore it is good tax planning to allocate property around the family in order to maximise the annual exemptions. For this to be effective, actual beneficial ownership of the property must pass to the children: it is not enough merely to put the property or other assets into their names.

Box 72 **OTHER EXEMPTIONS**
There are many items which are completely exempt from Capital Gains Tax and any gains or losses on them should not be included in the tax return. The list below is intended to be illustrative, not exhaustive.

Household goods, personal belongings and other chattels
These are normally completely exempt if each chattel is worth £3,000 or less at the time of both acquisition and disposal. If you sold a picture which had cost £1,000 for £2,500 the gain would be exempt. But if the picture had been sold for £10,000 the gain arising would be taxable as usual. There are special rules applying to the sale of sets of articles to the same 'connected' person. If you disposed of a set of six Chippendale chairs to your brother, with each chair perhaps realising a profit of £1,000, whereas the set together would have realised a gain of £15,000, and provided the disposals were made within a six-year period, the Revenue could amalgamate all the gains together to increase the total chargeable amount arising. They would do this by treating each sale as $\frac{1}{6}$ of the total value of the set.

Disposals up to a value of £3,000 are entirely exempt provided that the asset is not currency. If the consideration exceeds £3,000 the chargeable gain is limited to $\frac{5}{3}$ of the excess. Effectively, therefore, if you sell something which has cost £1,000 for £4,000 the $\frac{5}{3}$ rule would give a maximum capital gain of £1,666, whereas the actual capital gain which would have arisen would have been £3,000 before indexation relief.

Wasting Assets
Any disposal of a wasting asset (other than one on which you could have claimed capital allowances for trading purposes) is

exempt from Capital Gains Tax. This would include any asset which could not last more than fifty years and would always include items such as boats and planes. Someone who collected steam traction engines could sell them at a gain and there would be no taxable amount arising. If, however, he had a farming business and sold the tractor for an amount greater than he paid for it that would be a chargeable gain, as he could have claimed capital allowances on the tractor.

Private Cars
Private cars are always exempt from Capital Gains Tax so that if you buy and then sell a vintage Rolls Royce for more than you paid for it no capital gain arises and no tax will be incurred, unless you indulge in the activity to such an extent that it might be considered by the Revenue to be a trade, in which case Income Tax will arise on the profits being made.

Savings certificates, premium bonds and British savings bonds
These are exempt from tax.

Gilt Edged Securities
Irrespective of the length of ownership, any disposal of these assets is exempt from Capital Gains Tax so that any gain is not taxed and any loss is not allowable. This is completely different from the purchase and sale of shares, which always incurs tax.

Life assurance policies and deferred annuity contracts
As long as these were taken out by the person disposing of them there is no Capital Gains Tax. If, however, you buy a life assurance policy from someone else for cash or its equivalent value the disposal of that is chargeable as a capital gain.

Currency
Though the disposal and sale of a foreign currency can be charged to Capital Gains Tax, foreign currency acquired to meet personal or family expenditure abroad, such as the cost of a holiday, is exempt.

Compensation

If you receive compensation or damages for any wrong or injury suffered, perhaps in a car accident, then that is not taxable to capital gains.

Debts

A debt disposed of by the original creditor or his personal representative or legatee is exempt from Capital Gains Tax. This is not the position if you have acquired the debt from the original creditor for cash or its value and then disposed of it.

Decorations

The sale of a decoration for valour or gallantry is exempt, unless it had been acquired by the vendor for profit. This would cover for example the sale of a Victoria Cross.

Box 73 **DWELLING HOUSES**

Any gain to an individual on the disposal of an interest in a dwelling house which has been his only or main residence during his period of ownership is either fully or partly exempt from Capital Gains Tax. Though the gain is exempt you must give details of the disposal on the tax return.

If you have lived in a house as your principal private residence for any period the last two years of ownership are always treated as exempt. Suppose therefore you lived in a property for six months, let it for five and a half years and then sold it, the exempt period would be the initial half year period of residence plus the last two years, that is, two and a half years out of the total six-year period, so only the balance of the proportionate gain would be taxable. In addition there is a residential letting exemption of whichever is the greater of £20,000 or the exempt amount due, because you lived in the property at one stage.

It is always a good plan to ensure if you have more than one property that you are always able to claim some principal private residence exemption from Capital Gains Tax on each property. It is possible to elect in the first two years of having two properties (and they do not both have to be owned – one could be rented) which of the properties is to carry the exemption. In the first two years the right of election is the taxpayer's alone and cannot be challenged by the Revenue if both properties are residences. If the two-year period passes without an election then, subject to the Revenue allowing a late claim, it is up to the tax inspector to decide on the facts which one really was your main residence for Capital Gains Tax purposes.

It should be noted in this age of regular travel to Europe that the exemption can apply not just to houses in the UK but also to those abroad.

Dependent relatives' houses

If you own a private residence occupied by a dependent relative the gain arising on its disposal is exempt from Capital Gains Tax. Only one dependent resident's house may qualify for relief per claimant or per husband and wife. 'Dependent relative' is defined here as any relative of the taxpayer or his wife who is incapacitated by old age – over 64 – or infirmity from maintaining himself, or the mother of the taxpayer or his wife who, whether or not incapacitated, is either widowed or living apart from her husband or as a single woman in consequence of the dissolution or annulment of her marriage.

Following the considerable reduction in Capital Gains Tax from 6th April this relief is abolished. Transitional provisions will preserve the relief if the relative is in residence on the 5th April 1988 for the period up to when the dependent relative ceases to occupy the property. The relief will continue to be available for periods prior to 5th April 1988 during which the relative occupied the property.

Gifts relief

If you dispose of an asset to another party for less than its market value then you have made a full or partial gift. It is possible to hold over the part of the gain which applies to the gift element if both parties agree to the election. A gift may be to an individual resident in the UK or to the trustees of a settlement resident in the UK. If the individual were to become non-resident within a six-year period, still retaining the asset transferred, or if a trust was to become non-resident while still holding the asset, the capital gain originally held over could crystallise – that is, become taxable – except in certain restricted circumstances. If the gain should crystallise and the person to whom you had given the asset did not pay the tax owing, then the Revenue could look to you as the donor.

Business reliefs

There are various business reliefs available against Capital Gains Tax.

Rollover relief

If at any time during the course of a business assets are sold which have been used for the purposes of the trade and a capital gain arises, it is possible to rollover or transfer the capital gain by purchasing other assets for the purposes of that or another trade. The purchase must be made in the period from twelve months before the disposal which results in the gain to three years after the disposal. Suppose therefore a restauranteur sold his restaurant and two years later purchased a farm, he could rollover the capital gain from the restaurant into the farm. In order to qualify for full rollover relief he must spend at least the same amount out on the farm that he had received for the disposal of the restaurant. If he spends less, the part which has not been reinvested is chargeable to Capital Gains Tax up to the limit of the capital gain which would have arisen in the first place.

Similar reliefs are available where the individual making the disposal is selling an asset which has been used by his family company if he purchases another asset for that same company to use. If the asset being sold was owned by an employee of the company, there is an equivalent relief.

Retirement relief

Particularly valuable is retirement relief which is available at up to £125,000 in the 1987/88 tax year per individual so that both husband and wife can qualify. The relief is available in full on the disposal of part or all of a business or on the sale of shares in a family company. This is generally a company in which either you own 25 per cent of the shares or you hold 5 per cent and your family own a sufficient number that together with your own shares will take the total holdings over 50 per cent.

Before you can obtain full retirement relief the conditions required are:

● You must be over 60 when selling the shares or business.
● You must have owned the business or shares for ten years. Partial relief is available for at least one year of ownership.
● It is possible to obtain relief below the age of 60 if you are retiring early on medical grounds, but the Revenue will need convincing with medical support that the retirement is genuine and may well refer you to the Board's own medical officer. Anyone who thinks they can obtain this relief and then go and work elsewhere would be hard pressed to convince the Revenue of the validity of their claim.

It is possible to string together different businesses to build up the continuous ten-year period needed for maximum relief. So long as at least one year can be claimed you are entitled to some relief and every year completed gives 10 per cent of the total relief up to the maximum indicated of £125,000.

If you are over 60 it is not necessary actually to retire in order to obtain retirement relief and it is also possible to retire more than once within the overall limit of £125,000.

While for rollover relief it does not matter if you have obtained rent from a family company or a partnership, any such letting at commercial rental values would be disastrous in obtaining retirement relief, since the asset would then be regarded as an investment asset. In a company context where shares are being sold, any investment assets held by the company are also prejudicial to obtaining full relief. Therefore before the sale of shares in such a family trading company any investments held should be liquidated so that only cash is held by the company at the date of disposal of the shares. Cash is not counted as an investment asset.

The 1988 Finance Bill proposed an extension of the Capital Gains Tax retirement relief provisions. The position after 6th April 1988 is that retirement relief is an even more valuable form of

Example 1:

Mr A (age 65) disposes of his business, which he has been running for 20 years, on 1st May 1988. The gain after indexation is £250,000. He has had no earlier retirement relief.

Gain	£250,000
Amount available for full relief	£125,000
Amount available for 50% relief: £250,000–£125,000	£125,000
Amount of relief available: £125,000 + (50% × £125,000)	£187,500
Gain	£250,000
Less retirement relief	£187,500
Chargeable gain	£62,500

Example 2:

Mrs B (age 65) disposes of her business, which she has been running for 6 years, on 1st May 1988. The gain after indexation is £250,000. She has had no earlier retirement relief.

Gain	£250,000
Width of 'full relief band' £125,000 × 60%	£75,000
Upper limit of '50% relief band' (£500,000 × 60%) . .	£300,000
Amount available for full relief	£75,000
Amount available for 50% relief: £250,000–£75,000 . .	£175,000
Amount of relief available: £75,000 + (50% × £175,000)	£162,500
Gain	£250,000
Less retirement relief	£162,500
Chargeable gain	£87,500

relief than it was before that date. On top of the previous £125,000 it is proposed that exemption relief should be extended to 50 per cent of the gains between £125,000 and £500,000. This would only apply to disposals following 6th April 1988. The operation of the new provisions can best be illustrated by the two examples on page 119.

Compulsory Purchase

Rollover relief is extended to all landowners who dispose of land to authorities exercising compulsory powers if the landowners concerned reinvest part or the whole of the proceeds in acquiring new land. Again, relief is restricted if part only of the proceeds is reinvested.

The provisions for the acquisition of the new land are similar to the other rollover relief provisions.

Depreciating assets

These are assets which are either wasting assets at the time of acquisition or will become so within a period of ten years. Any leases on land which have less than sixty years to run will be depreciating assets. It is possible to hold over a capital gain by acquiring a depreciating asset, but you would not obtain full rollover relief. Under the hold over relief provisions the capital gain held over will crystallise at the earliest of the following occasions.

- After 10 years.
- At the disposal of the assets.
- When they cease to be used for the trade.

If before any of these events occur a further asset is acquired which is not a depreciating asset, the trader may claim rollover relief as if the third asset had been purchased when the original asset was sold.

In appropriate circumstances the three-year limit referred to on page 117 for rollover relief can be increased up to ten years.

Incorporation relief

If a business is incorporated in exchange for shares then the capital gain arising on the disposal of the business can be rolled over into the cost of the shares. This assumes that all the assets and liabilities of the business (other than cash) are taken over.

There is separate relief for making gifts of business assets to a company. If you transfer the goodwill of your business into a company you already own there would be no capital gain arising because of this relief.

Share-for-share exchanges and reorganisations

Any reorganisation of a company's share capital or exchange of one share for another in a takeover situation is usually exempt from Capital Gains Tax and it is possible to rollover the cost of the original shares into the second parcel of shares acquired. When you eventually dispose of the shares newly acquired to find out the gain the base cost of the original asset is set against the final disposal proceeds.

MISCELLANEOUS RELIEFS

Assets given to charities and other national bodies

There is a special relief provided if you give assets to a charity or to any of the bodies mentioned under the taxing statutes. These include the National Gallery, the British Museum, the National Museum of Wales and any local authority and any government department. In such circumstances if the asset is gifted the only capital gain that will be charged is the amount of money received over the cost allowable under the ordinary Capital Gains Tax rules.

Loans to traders

If you make a loan to a trader for use in his business and eventually that loan is not repaid or not repaid in full the loss arising is eligible for Capital Gains Tax relief. Similarly if you guarantee a loan made to a trader you are entitled to capital loss to the extent that the guarantee is called upon.

Box 74 HOW TO CALCULATE A GAIN OR LOSS

As detailed above, when the whole of an asset is disposed of the gain is relatively straightforward to calculate. But when there is a partial disposal of an asset, for example the sale of part of a piece of land, the acquisition cost which can be attributed to the part sold is in general that portion of the cost of the whole asset which is represented by the fraction $\frac{A}{A+B}$, where A equals the proceeds of the part disposal and B is the market value of the part retained at the time of the disposal.

In the case of a succession of part disposals the $A/A+B$ formula would be used on each occasion. As indicated on page 121 shares have their own special rules using pooling rather than the $A/A+B$ formula.

Box 75   ASSETS HELD ON 6 APRIL 1965

For years prior to 6th April 1988 only gains after 6th April 1965 are taxable. With unquoted shares or land without development value you can elect that instead of time apportioning the gain you can take the value at 6th April 1965 as the base cost for Capital Gains Tax. After 6th April 1988 assets are rebased on their 31st March 1982 value if owned before that date.

Box 76   BUSINESS EXPANSION SCHEME SHARES

Disposal of business expansion scheme shares are exempt from Capital Gains Tax. They must be held for five years if the Income Tax reliefs obtainable when the shares are first acquired are not to be lost.

NON-RESIDENT COMPANIES

If a non-resident company sells assets in the UK then it will not be liable to Capital Gains Tax since this only applies to companies who are either resident or ordinarily resident in the UK. However, if the company is non-UK resident its beneficial shareholders can have the capital gain apportioned to them according to the proportion of the shares they own in that company. So if Mr A, living in the the UK, owns 10 per cent of the shares of XYZ Limited, a company registered in, and controlled from, Jersey, and XYZ Limited makes a capital gain of £50,000, Mr A would be chargeable on a £5,000 gain whether or not he receives any money from XYZ Limited.

NON-RESIDENT SETTLEMENT

Non-resident settlements, like non-resident companies, are not liable to UK Capital Gains Tax. Unlike non-resident companies, however, any gain arising is not apportioned out to beneficiaries unless those beneficiaries receive payment. If they do then they are taxable under Capital Gains Tax if the trust has already made a capital gain. If, for example, the trust makes a capital gain in year one of £50,000 and three UK resident beneficiaries receive £10,000 each in year four, they would be taxable on £10,000 each in year four. So long as the money stays outside the UK they are not liable.

BONUS ISSUES

These are not charged to Capital Gains Tax and the shares acquired are simply added to the pool of shares so that the average cost of the share is diminished by the increase in the total number.

ASSETS QUALIFYING FOR CAPITAL ALLOWANCES

When these assets are disposed of there can be a capital gain just as with any other asset if they raise more than the original cost. The chattels exemption does not apply. However, if the assets are disposed of for less than the acquisition cost, no capital loss will be available for relief because the taxpayer would already have received Income Tax relief under the capital allowances rules by way of a balancing allowance.

HUSBAND TO WIFE TRANSFERS

These are exempt and continue to be exempt even in the year of separation up to the 5th April. In years following that in which separation occurs, however, there is no exemption and capital gains can arise. It is also unlikely that the gifts relief would apply in a divorce situation where a husband may transfer property to his wife. You must therefore take great care in such circumstances that you are aware of the taxation consequences of any disposals.

INTERACTION OF MAIN RESIDENCE EXEMPTION AND ROLLOVER RELIEFS

It is apparent that there are many circumstances where there can be rollover relief on the transfer of assets from one person to another, or indeed from a trust to a beneficiary. If the person who has received the asset uses it for a purpose which is exempt from Capital Gains Tax, for example to buy a main private residence, then when he sells that asset, even if the period of ownership is only six months, the entire capital gain is exempt from tax and not just that portion which relates to that period of ownership.

If a property had been in trust for ten years and a gain of £100,000 had built up from the base cost of £20,000, and that asset was transferred to a beneficiary of the trust who used it as his main home, then the beneficiary would take over the base cost of £20,000. If the property was subsequently sold for £140,000 the entire gain of £120,000 would be exempt because of the period of residence.

Such reliefs are also available where a father might transfer an investment property to a child for that child to live in. Any subsequent disposal by the child would take into account the father's deemed acquisition cost but would have full Capital Gains Tax exemption on the gain arising.

Box 77   OFFSHORE FUNDS

Until recently offshore funds were popular as tax avoidance schemes. People were encouraged to convert what would have been an Income Tax charge into a Capital Gains Tax charge with the intention of using the CGT exemption. These advantages have largely or totally been removed and any gain is likely to be subject to Income Tax.

If you are in doubt as to how the profit arising should be taxed you should either refer back to the offshore funds administrators for their advice or give the details to the tax inspector dealing with your affairs so that he may advise you.

Box 78   PERSONAL EQUITY PLANS (PEPs)

Personal equity plans were introduced in the 1986 Finance Act, to encourage direct investment in UK companies. Investment in a plan builds up entirely free of Income Tax (on reinvested dividends) and Capital Gains Tax, so long as it is retained in the plan for at least a complete calendar year after the year in which the investment is made.

Investors do not need to keep records, or declare their dividends and gains on their tax returns – hence a personal equity plan does not involve the Inland Revenue at all. The administration is carried out by an authorised plan manager. Investors may put a lump sum into a plan, or invest a regular amount. They must subscribe to a 'discretionary' plan where the plan manager makes the investment decisions or a non-discretionary one where the investor decides what shares to buy.

Inland Revenue figures are now available for plans started in 1987, the first year of operation of the scheme: these show that over 250,000 people invested nearly £500 million.

Box 79 **PERSONS CHARGEABLE**

Withdrawals from a personal equity plan into which you can invest up to £3,000 per annum may be liable to Income Tax and Capital Gains Tax if the rules of the scheme have not been fully followed.

Until 6th April 1990 the gains and losses of a husband and wife are combined in a net charge made upon the husband. If separate assessment as detailed on page 111 is required the Revenue will supply form CG11S on request.

Trustees of a settlement are responsible for making an annual return of the trust's capital gains and any trustee who has not made a return should request a tax form from the Revenue district dealing with the trust.

Box 80 **TAX CHARGEABLE**

The Capital Gains Tax rate prior to 6th April 1988 after the annual exemption was at 30 per cent for individuals and at a variable rate of between 27 and 35 per cent for companies. The 30 per cent rate had been unchanged for individuals since the inception of capital gains in 1965.

AVOIDANCE OF CAPITAL GAINS TAX

There is no easy way to avoid Capital Gains Tax while you are resident in the United Kingdom. However, it is possible to avoid it by becoming non-resident and non-ordinarily resident in the United Kingdom before making the capital gain. If you have a large holding of shares or property and consider that it is worthwhile in personal terms, you can take steps to become non-resident before selling off the shares or land or whatever it may be. If this is done properly (and you will need good advice on how to go about it) then the entire charge on capital gains can be avoided in the United Kingdom.

It should be stressed that this is only in the United Kingdom and it must always be remembered that it can be a case of out of the frying pan and into the fire – other countries also have a similar tax and they may be better or worse than that of the UK. Those who have Spain in mind should beware: Spain's tax is more costly than the United Kingdom's.

There are various countries closer to hand, however, which have no Capital Gains Tax and those that immediately come to mind would be the Isle of Man, Jersey, Guernsey, Alderney and Gibraltar.

Box 81   RELIEF FOR INVESTMENT IN CORPORATE TRADES

This is commonly known as the business expansion scheme. So long as you subscribe at least £500 for shares in a qualifying company then you will obtain full Income Tax relief on the money invested. The limit is £40,000 per individual (or married couple) per year. The company must be a qualifying company and there are various restrictions on the trades which it may undertake and also on the relationship which the individuals investing may have to that company.

In general the Revenue is unhappy with companies which are heavily asset backed or which specialise in financial activities. It is possible to appeal against the Revenue's refusal to accept that a company qualifies for business expansion scheme relief and the writer has recently had a successful decision from the Special Commissioners on whether a recording studio company qualified for relief or not. From 5th April 1988 the qualifying company can be one letting residential properties on assured tenancies.

· 12 ·
INHERITANCE TAX

While not strictly within the terms of an Income Tax return, it seems relevant at this point to mention Inheritance Tax. This is a tax on either lifetime transfers or transfers on death.

During your lifetime you can make three sorts of transfer. In addition, certain transfers of excluded property are outside the scope of Inheritance Tax.

1. CHARGEABLE TRANSFER
A chargeable transfer is normally one made to a discretionary trust. A transfer made to an accumulation and maintenance trust or to a trust drawn up on an interest in possession basis would form a potentially exempt transfer.

2. POTENTIALLY EXEMPT TRANSFERS
This is a transfer between two individuals or between an individual and an interest in possession trust or between an individual and an accumulation and maintenance trust. The transfer is described as potentially exempt because it is only fully exempt if the donor lives for a period of seven years from the date of transfer. Inside that period there is a tapering relief. The table is shown below.

Potentially exempt transfer table

Years between gift and death	Percentage of the full tax payable
Up to 3 years	100%
More than 3 but less than 4	80%
More than 4 but less than 5	60%
More than 5 but less than 6	40%
More than 6 but less than 7	20%

3. GIFTS WITH RESERVATION OF INTEREST

Any gift made with a reservation of interest is not a transfer of value when made but can be when the reservation of interest ceases. If, for example, you give a house to your son but reserve the right to live in it following the gift, then the value of the house is still in your estate so long as that reservation of interest is maintained. When the reservation ceases the transfer would then become a potentially exempt transfer and the seven-year clock would start running.

CHARGEABLE AMOUNTS

Each individual has an Inheritance Tax threshold before any chargeable transfer can mean tax will actually have to be paid. The threshold was £90,000 for 1987/88 up to the 15th March 1988. After that date the threshold was lifted to £110,000.

In calculating whether any tax is due, the latest chargeable transfer is added to the chargeable transfers made in the previous seven years and if the threshold limit is reached then the tax due is calculated from the Inheritance Tax table shown on page 00 for chargeable lifetime transfers. If the limit is not breached then no tax will be due. If tax was due on an earlier occasion then this must be taken into account in calculating how much tax will be due on the latest chargeable occasion.

There are annual exemptions on gifts of up to £3,000 per year available to a husband and wife and you are allowed to use the previous year's £3,000 exemption if that was not used at that time. Gifts which are part of your normal income expenditure are not chargeable transfers, although the gifts must not reduce your living standards. Gifts to people getting married, with a maximum of £5,000 from a parent, £2,500 from a grandparent and £1,000 from anybody else, are allowed over and above the £3,000 limit. Small gifts of up to £250 per recipient p.a. are also exempt.

On death there is a 'Death Rate' table used to calculate how much Inheritance Tax is due based on the value of the assets held at death. Gifts between husband and wife are exempt from Inheritance Tax. Transfers to others are chargeable. Added to the value of the estate are any other chargeable transfers made in the last seven years and also any potential exempt transfers in accordance with the table on page 127. The total value represents the full value of the estate and the tax bill can be worked out from the tables on pages 130 and 131.

BUSINESS RELIEFS
There are two important reliefs from Inheritance Tax which can reduce the amount of tax payable. These are business property relief and agricultural property relief. They allow you to reduce the amount to be included in your estate for Inheritance Tax by taking into account the value of a business or assets of that business or shares held in either a quoted or unquoted company, depending on the size of the holding. The relief varies between 30 and 50 per cent of the total value depending on the exact circumstances and size of the holding.

LOSS TO DONOR PRINCIPLE
For Inheritance Tax it is not the value of the actual asset transferred that counts but the difference in the value of the donor's estate before and after giving the asset. If, therefore, a donor is giving away 49 per cent of the 100 per cent of shares he owns in a company, then the difference value of 100 per cent of the company and 51 per cent of the company is the measure of the loss to his estate, and that is the value of the transfer for Inheritance Tax purposes.

TAX TIP
It will be seen from the tables below on pages 130 and 131 that each person has the advantage of a large amount before coming into the maximum rate of Inheritance Tax. It is therefore an advantage for both husband and wife to equalise their estates in order to ensure the minimum amount of Inheritance Tax. Since husband and wife transfers are exempt, any assets which carry business or agricultural property relief should be transferred not to each other but to someone for whom the transfer would be chargeable, such as the children.

It should also be noted that any insurance policies relating to the life of the deceased should be written in trust so that the proceeds are paid not to the deceased's estate but instead to a beneficiary. In that way no Inheritance Tax will be due on the sum received.

Table 1

Transfers on death after 16th March 1987 but before 15th March 1988

Tax on transfers

	Gross taxable transfers £	Gross cumulative totals £	Rate	Equal to tax of £	Cumulative totals Taxable transfers £	Tax thereon £
First	90,000	0– 90,000	Nil	Nil	90,000	Nil
Next	50,000	90,001–140,000	30%	15,000	140,000	15,000
Next	80,000	140,001–220,000	40%	32,000	220,000	47,000
Next	110,000	220,001–330,000	50%	55,000	330,000	102,000
Above 330,000			60%			

Table 2

Chargeable lifetime transfers after 16th March 1987 but before 15th March 1988

Tax on gross transfers

	Gross taxable transfers £	Gross cumulative totals £	Rate	Equal to tax of £	Cumulative totals Taxable transfers £	Tax thereon £
First	90,000	0– 90,000	Nil	Nil	90,000	Nil
Next	50,000	90,001–140,000	15%	7,500	140,000	7,500
Next	80,000	140,001–220,000	20%	16,000	220,000	23,500
Next	110,000	220,001–330,000	25%	27,500	330,000	51,000
Above 330,000			30%			

Table 3

Transfers on death on or after 15th March 1988

Gross taxable transfer £	Gross cumulative total £	Rate £	Tax £	Cumulative Taxable transfers £	Total tax £
First 110,000	0–110,000	Nil	Nil	110,000	Nil
Balance		40%			

Table 4

Chargeable lifetime transfers on or after 15th March 1988

Gross taxable transfer £	Gross cumulative total £	Rate £	Tax £	Cumulative Taxable transfers £	Total tax £
First 110,000	0–110,000	Nil	Nil	110,000	Nil
Balance		20%			

A COMMON PROBLEM

One of the chief requirements in planning for Inheritance Tax is to transfer a property owned by an older member of the family, such as a father, to a younger member. It is not possible under the rules, as it was under the Capital Transfer Tax rules, for a father to live in the property having transferred its value. This is regarded as a reservation of interest and means that the entire value of the property is included in the father's estate at death.

One possible way out of this is for the father to grant a 10- to 20-year lease to himself before transferring the freehold reversion to his son, although there is a legal doubt as to whether you can grant a lease to yourself. This ensures that the value of the house is split, and that the father's estate is credited only with the value of the leasehold interest which diminishes as the years go by. This method is considered safer than granting a lifetime interest to the father, since a lifetime interest is likely to be regarded as an interest in possession and valued as if it were the entire property, giving no saving in Inheritance Tax.

TAX PLANNING

Assuming that Inheritance Tax planning takes place at least seven years before one's likely death, it should be possible eventually to pay no Inheritance Tax at all, or at least to restrict severely the amount due. If, however, you leave it until you are on your death bed there is effectively no method of saving Inheritance Tax other than marrying someone right away, since the only relief available is likely to be a husband-to-wife transfer. The various insurance-based schemes which previously provided relief from the worst aspects of Capital Transfer Tax are now considered to be largely ineffective, whatever their promoters may suggest.

GIFTS TO CHARITIES

It is possible to make a donation to a charity either during one's life or at death and to have that amount completely exempt from Inheritance Tax.

GIFTS TO POLITICAL PARTIES

After 15th March 1988 the previous £100,000 limit under which one might make an exempt transfer to a qualifying political party is abolished so that now political parties and charities have exactly the same rules. A political party is eligible for the exemption if, at the last general election before the gift, two members of that party were elected to the House of Commons, or one member was elected and at least 150,000 votes were cast in the party's favour.

· 13 ·
ALLOWANCES

The main allowances which are available for the 1986/87, 1987/88 and 1988/89 years of assessment are shown below:

PERSONAL ALLOWANCES

Allowance

	1986–87 £	1987–88 £	1988–89 £
Single person	2,335	2,425	2,605
Married man	3,655	3,795	4,095
Wife's earned income	2,335	2,425	2,605
Additional personal	1,320	1,370	1,490
Widow's bereavement	1,320	1,370	1,490
Blind person	360	540	540
Age – Single person (Age 65–79)	2,850	2,960	3,180
***Age – Single person (Age 80 and over)**	–	3,070	3,310
Age – Married man (Age 65–79)	4,505	4,675	5,035
***Age – Married man (Age 80 and over)**	–	4,845	5,205
Income limit for full age allowance	9,400	9,800	10,600

From 1987–88 a new, higher level of age allowance for those aged 80 and over was introduced. Subject to the income limit, you may be entitled to claim this allowance for 1987–88 if you (or in the case of a married man, either you or your wife) will be aged 80 years or over on 5th April 1988.

Allowances: Claim for year 6 April 1988 to 5 April 1989
Before making any claim, please read the appropriate note. Tick the box which applies and give the information asked for

83 ☐ **Married man's allowance** To claim this you must be living with or wholly maintaining your wife

Wife's first name(s)

If you were married after 5 April 1987, give — **both** Date of marriage **and** Wife's former surname

84 ☐ **Age allowance** To claim this you or your wife must have been born before 6 April 1924

85 ☐ **Additional personal allowance**

Child's name (Surname first)

Child's date of birth

If the child was 16 or over on 6 April 1988 and receiving full time education or training, give the name of the university, college, school or type of training.

Does he or she live with you? Yes ☐ No ☐

Is any other person claiming the allowance for the child? Yes ☐ No ☐

If you are claiming because your wife is unable to look after herself, what is her illness or disability?

Is she likely to be unable to look after herself throughout the year ending 5 April 1989? Yes ☐ No ☐

Box 83 *MARRIED MAN'S ALLOWANCE*

In order to claim married man's allowance a husband must be living with or wholly maintaining his wife. It is possible to obtain a married man's allowance even if a couple are separated and the husband is wholly maintaining the wife by voluntary contributions. No allowance is due, however, if payments are made under a court order or other legally binding agreement.

In the year of marriage the amount of the allowance received is reduced by $\frac{1}{12}$ of the difference between the married man's allowance and the single person's allowance for each month of the tax year which has passed prior to the date of marriage. So if you married on the 25th of October 1987 the relief would not be the full £3,795 but rather £3,795 less $\frac{6}{12} \times £1,370 = £3,110$. The tax return should show the wife's first name and her former surname, and the date of marriage if that was after the beginning of the year covered by the tax return.

The married man's allowance is not available if a wife's earnings election is in force (see pages 16–20). If a man is in possession of an additional personal allowance (see Box 85 pages 135–136) then it is better not to claim a married man's allowance in the year of marriage, since these allowances are mutually exclusive. But where a married man's allowance is reduced (if the marriage does not take place in the first month of the tax year) an additional personal allowance is paid in full if it is due at any time of the tax year.

In the year of divorce a full married man's allowance may be claimed since there is no restriction to the allowance in the year of separation as there is in the year of marriage.

Box 84 *AGE ALLOWANCE*

As the table on page 133 shows, age allowance provides a considerably increased tax allowance for those aged over 65, with one rate being payable between 65 and 80 and another for those aged 80 and over. There is both a single and a married rate of the allowance in each age band. If therefore you are 65 in the year covered by the tax return, then you should claim the age allowance in that period. Once claimed, the Revenue should automatically include it in your assessment or coding notice each year, but you should always check that this has been done.

There is an age allowance clawback for those whose income is above the threshold figure shown in the table. The age allowance is reduced by £2 for every £3 of excess income. Since the income will also be taxed to at least the basic rate of tax, this provides an actual marginal rate of tax of 45 per cent in 1987/88 and 41.67% in 1988/89. As the income goes above the threshold figure the benefit of age allowance is progressively lost, but the clawback cannot reduce the personal reliefs to an amount below the normal figures for single or married person's allowance. Those within the age allowance clawback trap for 1988/89 have the dubious privilege of paying the UK's highest marginal rate of tax.

Box 85 *ADDITIONAL PERSONAL ALLOWANCE*

Arithmetically this is the difference between a single person's allowance and a married person's allowance. It may only be claimed if you satisfy the conditions below and cannot claim a married man's allowance (not simply that you choose not to claim the married man's allowance), or if you are a married man whose wife is unable to look after herself throughout the next tax year because of permanent illness or disablement. The conditions are that there is a child living with you who is either your own (including a stepchild or a legally adopted child) or any other child under eighteen years of age on 6th April 1988 who is maintained at your own expense. Typical claimants of an additional personal allowance are widows, widowers and single parents.

To claim for a child over eighteen, the child must be in full-time education or on at least a two-year training course for a trade or profession.

The additional personal allowance is per child, subject to the fact that one claimant may only have one allowance. Where there has been a divorce with more than one child involved, each parent may claim an additional personal allowance if the above rules apply to them.

The Revenue are relatively generous in interpreting the 'living with' condition and a father who has his children living with him for all or part of the school holidays would be regarded as qualifying for an additional personal allowance if he was not already claiming married man's allowance from a second marriage. The ex-wife could claim an additional personal allowance for the second child. But if there is only one child of the marriage only one allowance can be shared between both parents and if the allowance claim is disputed this can be divided between them on an agreed or apportioned basis.

It has not been possible to claim both the additional personal allowance and the housekeeper allowance referred to below on pages 141–142.

The questions on the tax return are designed to ensure that all the information is available to the Revenue when the claim is made. Boxes should be filled in factually, bearing in mind the criteria set out above.

CHANGES TO ADDITIONAL PERSONAL ALLOWANCE PROPOSED IN 1988 FINANCE BILL

Where an unmarried couple have two or more children resident with them they can each claim an additional personal allowance. This is on top of the single person's allowance. Between them, the couple qualify for a substantially higher tax allowance total than a married couple with the same children. It is therefore intended to change from 6th April 1989 the qualifying conditions for the additional personal allowance so that an unmarried couple living together as husband and wife with children can claim no more than one additional personal allowance between them. Other claimants for the additional personal allowance will not be affected by these changes.

86	☐ **Dependent relative allowance**	What is the dependant's annual income (excluding voluntary contributions) from:	
	Dependant's name	State pension or benefit	£
	Dependant's date of birth	Other pension	£
	Does he or she live with you? Yes ☐ No ☐	Other income	£
	What is the dependant's relationship to you or your wife (if mother, say if widowed, divorced or separated)?	If the dependant does not live with you, enter the weekly amount you contribute	£
	What is the dependant's illness or disability (if any)?	If any other relative contributes, enter the weekly amount contributed	£
87	☐ **Blind person's allowance** Local Authority or equivalent body with which registered and the date of registration — *say if self or wife*		

Box 86   *DEPENDENT RELATIVE ALLOWANCE*

The entry on the 1988/89 tax return should be ignored since this allowance has been abolished from 6th April 1988. However, details of the allowance up to this date are given here, as you have six years in which to make a late claim.

The amount of this allowance was comparatively small at £100. In order to claim it you had to show that you were maintaining either a relative of the taxpayer or of his wife who was unable to work because of old age or permanent illness or disablement, or your mother or mother-in-law who was separated, divorced or widowed.

Relief was available for each relative who came within the required category. If the relative's own income exceeded the basic retirement pension by more than £100 then no relief was available. For a female claimant (taxed separately) the allowance was £145 and again if income exceeded the basic retirement pension by more than this no relief was due.

Where two or more people maintained a dependent relative the relief was split between them in proportion to their payments for the relative's keep.

This relief was likely to benefit very few people and even when available in full the tax saving was miserly. The definition of old age for Revenue purposes is 64 or over before the start of the tax year. In order to get any allowance at all the Revenue require that at least £75 must be contributed.

Box 87   *BLIND PERSON'S ALLOWANCE*

Claims may be made if either the taxpayer or his wife is a registered blind person. If both are registered blind two allowances are due. It is not possible to obtain both this allowance and the son or daughter's service allowance referred to in Box 89, abolished since 6th April 1988. If both are applicable the blind person's allowance is given in preference since it is considerably larger. In order to claim you should simply indicate the local authority or equivalent body with whom you are registered and give the date of registration indicating if the claim is made on behalf of yourself or your wife.

WIDOW'S BEREAVEMENT ALLOWANCES

A widow is entitled in the year of bereavement and the following year to an additional allowance of an amount equivalent to the additional personal allowance. In the year after that of bereavement the relief is available only if the widow has not remarried. The allowance is given in addition to all other reliefs. There is no comparable relief for widowers.

Allowances: Claim for year 6 April 1988 to 5 April 1989

88	☐ **Retirement annuity payments**	Contract or scheme membership number
	Enter the nature of your trade, profession or employment **unless** your earnings come from a non-pensionable employment where you should give the name of your employer.	
		Amount paid in the year to 5 April 1988 £
	Name of Insurance Company, etc or trust scheme	Amount to be paid in the year to 5 April 1989 £
		Enter your date of birth
		If you require a special form, enter an 'X' here ▶ ☐

To claim any of the following allowances, tick the box that applies and I will send you the appropriate claim form.

89-91	☐ Son or daughter whose services you depend on	☐ Housekeeper allowance	☐ Friendly Society and Trade Union Death and Superannuation benefits

Box 88 *RETIREMENT ANNUITY PAYMENTS*

These are a form of pension relief for those who are not in employers' pension schemes. The self-employed can benefit from retirement annuity schemes and those who are in non-pensionable employment. Retirement annuities are a very good way of saving tax and up to certain limits you can obtain 100 per cent tax deduction on the sums paid into a qualifying retirement annuity scheme.

The limits are defined as a percentage of net relevant earnings dependent upon age:

Age at beginning of year of assessment	Percentage net relevant earnings eligible for relief
Age up to 50	17½%
51–55	20%
56–60	22.5%
61 or more	27.5%

These are the maximum amounts on which you may obtain relief and if you pay premiums higher than these percentages of net relevant earnings in any year then any excess premium paid may not be carried forward. You must be careful therefore not to pay more than you can claim relief for in a year. It is possible to bring forward unused relief from previous years, so that if for example you had been able to pay £1,000 per year premium in each of the last four years and had chosen not to, you could now make a payment in this year. It would be possible to pay a total premium of £5,000 and obtain relief.

Another useful facility is that you may make a payment in 1987/88 and before the 5th April 1988 elect to have relief set against income for the previous year instead of 1987/88. This ensures that relief is claimed at the highest percentage rate of tax rather than the lower rates which you might be paying in a subsequent year. It is understood that as a concession the

Revenue may extend the 5th April deadline for the election by three months.

When electing to claim retirement annuity relief in an earlier year it may be that there were no net relevant earnings that year. If so you may go back one further period in order to obtain relief. There is no necessity that there be any net relevant earnings in the year in which the premium is actually paid, so the payment carried back could be made two years after you had actually ceased having relevant earnings. Unused relief may be carried forward for up to six years on a first in, first out basis against a premium paid in a subsequent year. Relief of past years brought forward is only relevant to the extent that the maximum percentage limits of net relevant earnings in the year in which the premiums are paid are exceeded.

The majority of insurance companies have retirement annuity schemes and they are often called Section 226 Policies from the section of the Taxes Act 1970 from which they take their validity. It should always be remembered that retirement annuities are a form of investment for your old age and when choosing with which insurance company to invest your savings, it is important to consider carefully the standing and past record of that company.

You will see that there is no space on the form to claim for any retirement annuity payments made by your wife. These can either be squeezed in outside the Box or a separate schedule can be attached to the form together with an explanatory note.

The insurance company concerned will supply its clients with a form SEPC which is the certificate the Revenue require if you are to obtain relief. These forms should be carefully filed before sending them to the Revenue as they are very valuable.

It is possible to ask the Revenue to include in your tax coding notice an estimate for the amount of retirement annuity likely to be paid in the year before actually submitting the certificates to them. This ensures that you will obtain tax relief at the same time as you are making the payments.

NET RELEVANT EARNINGS
The amount of net relevant earnings that you have decides how much retirement annuity relief you are entitled to. Net relevant

earnings means earnings from non-pensionble employment or from businesses, profession or partnerships. They are reduced by any losses arising from a business which would otherwise produce net relevant earnings. Claims to items such as 100 per cent industrial building allowances for investments in enterprise zones or for business expansion schemes relief on investments in qualifying companies may reduce your taxable earnings but do not reduce the net relevant earnings, since income from the industrial buildings or the shares would be investment income and that can never count as relevant earnings.

SECTION 226A RELIEF

There is a form of life assurance relief under the retirement annuities legislation which provides full tax relief on up to 5 per cent of your net relevant earnings for policies paid where the main aim is to provide an income for your widow or dependents or a lump sum after your death. Any premiums paid on the life insurance policies count towards the overall $17\frac{1}{2}$ per cent or higher limits, but you do gain tax relief on the full premium paid on the life assurance policy.

Box 89 SON'S OR DAUGHTER'S SERVICES

The entry on the 1988/89 tax return should be ignored since this allowance has been abolished from 6th April 1988. As with the dependent relative allowance, however, you have up to six years in which to make a late claim for a previous year. The details of the allowance which was relevant up to 6th April 1988 are therefore given.

A small allowance could be claimed if the taxpayer was maintaining his son or daugher and he or she was living with him and looking after him or his wife because he was old (over 64) or permanently ill or disabled. It was not possible to have both this allowance and the housekeeper allowance, and if you qualified for both the housekeeper allowance should be claimed as it was the larger. The housekeeper allowance was also abolished from 6th April 1988.

Box 90 HOUSEKEEPER ALLOWANCE

The housekeeper allowance was abolished from 6th April 1988 and therefore the entry on the tax return for this should be ignored.

You could make a claim for this allowance if you were a widow or widower and your housekeeper lived in. If the housekeeper was a relative, any other taxpayer who could claim tax allowances for that person had to give them up before the claim could be accepted. It would not be possible, for instance, to claim for a related housekeeper who was married, since her husband could claim a married man's allowance for her.

If the housekeeper was not a relative, it was required that the person be employed by the taxpayer for the purpose claimed. It was not possible to claim both this allowance and the additional personal allowance. If both were available you would claim the additional personal allowance, which was larger. The additional personal allowance is also available after 6th April 1988.

INDEPENDENT TAXATION

It is proposed that a new system of independent taxation will come into being in April 1990. As detailed earlier this will mean that married women will, for the first time, be completely independent of their husbands for tax purposes. It will also mean that there will be a new personal allowance for everyone, male or female, married or single, which can be set against all types of income. There will, therefore, be no single person's allowance. The new personal allowance is intended to be equal to the old single person's allowance.

There will also be a married couple's allowance equivalent to the difference under the old system between the married allowance and the single allowance. So the new tax system will continue to recognise marriage. The new allowance will go to the husband unless he has insufficient income to use it himself, in which case any unused part can be transferred to his wife. Since the personal allowance and the married couple's allowance will together be equal to the married man's allowance under the old system, a married man will suffer no reduction in his tax threshold.

There will be larger personal and married couple's allowances for elderly taxpayers aged 65 to 79 or 80 and over. Elderly married women will qualify for age allowance in their own right for the first time.

TRANSFER OF MARRIED COUPLE'S ALLOWANCE
The new married couple's allowance will go to the husband in the first instance. If he cannot make full use of it he will be able to transfer the unused part to his wife. This ensures that a couple where the wife is the sole earner will have the same allowances as a couple where the husband is the sole earner.

MORTGAGE INTEREST RELIEF
Under the old system married couples shared the £30,000 limit. Mortgage interest relief under the new provisions is allowable whether the eligible loan was made to the husband or the wife or jointly to both, and whether the interest is paid by the husband or wife.

Where one spouse pays tax at a higher marginal rate than the other it will be possible to make an election to allocate the eligible relief to the first partner and so ensure that it is all allowable at the highest rate. This allows for great flexibility, and also ensures that no problem arises, say, from the husband claiming relief when the interest is being paid out of a joint bank account.

DISADVANTAGED COUPLES
The losers of the new allowances system to come in on 6th April 1990 are the couples where the wife works and the husband stays at home, having no earned income. In such circumstances it is possible at present to transfer the full married man's allowance to the wife so that she has two allowances to set against her income. From 6th April 1990 this will not be possible, and only the new married couple's allowance will be transferable.

Box 91   DEATH, SICKNESS AND SUPERANNUATION BENEFITS
This entry claims for certain payments to a friendly society on combined policies providing both sickness and death benefits

which are not within life assurance or superannuation arrangements made by your employer or by the life assurance company or the friendly society itself. Relief is also available for the proportion of a trade union subscription which relates to superannuation and life assurance or funeral benefits.

92	☐ **Life assurance-limits to relief**
	If in the year ended 5 April 1988 you and/or your wife paid more than — £1275 in life assurance premiums (including £85 in deferred annuity premiums and compulsory deferred annuity premiums) payments to provide annuities for *enter the total paid* £ _____ widows and orphans *enter the total paid* £ _____
93	☐ **Personal pension plans** If you pay contributions to a personal pension scheme or receive tax relief at source for contributions you pay to a scheme separate from your employer's pension scheme, enter an "X" here ▶ ☐

Box 92 *LIFE ASSURANCE RELIEF LIMITS*

No relief is due on any life assurance policy taken out or enhanced after 13th March 1984, but if payments are being made on policies enacted before that date, the total of the premiums or relative payments which qualify for relief are limited to the greater of £1,500 gross premium or $\frac{1}{6}$ of total income. Any payments made above these levels would therefore be denied tax relief. There are also limits of £100 for the amount of deferred annuity premiums and compulsory payments to provide annuities for widows and orphans.

Any tax relief due is given at source by the life insurance company. The rate of premium relief is reduced to 12.5 per cent from 6th April 1989. All you have to do is to enter on the tax return the amount paid and the Revenue will make any restriction necessary in the tax assessment.

Box 93 *PERSONAL PENSION PLANS*

Personal pension plans were intended to come into operation with effect from 4th January 1988. To a large extent the new contracts replace and resemble closely retirement annuity plans. It will not be possible to enter into a retirement annuity contract after personal pensions come into being, but those with plans already in existence may continue them. Personal pensions have been put back six months and they now come into force on 1st July 1988.

Tax relief will be given at source by basic rate tax being deducted on personal pension payments. Higher-rate relief will also be available. Once the provisions come into force you will be required to put an 'X' at the relevant point on the tax return. The Revenue will send a separate form so that you can claim the relevant higher-rate relief if appropriate.

Declaration

False statements can result in prosecution

To the best of my knowledge and belief, the particulars given on this form are correct and complete

A woman should state after her signature whether she is single, married, widowed, separated or divorced	
Signature	Date

If you are making the return as executor, trustee, receiver, factor, etc give the capacity in which you act and for whom the return is made.

Private address use CAPITAL letters		Please enter your National Insurance number if it is not already shown on the front of this form
	Postcode	

If there is any other information which you think may affect your income tax liability, please give details on a separate piece of paper.

THE DECLARATION

The final entry on the tax return is the declaration and you should always carefully note the warning that you have filled in the tax return to the '*best of one's knowledge and belief*' and that the particulars given on the form are correct and complete. The warning that false statements can result in prosecution is not meant to put the fear of God into the taxpayer but rather to stress that the tax return is a serious matter. You are guaranteeing that the entries are correct as far as you know, and so at least moderate care should have been taken to ensure that this is true.

You should not sign a tax return until all the entries are completed and only when you are certain that everything required has been returned, in order to give the Revenue the opportunity to assess the correct amount of tax due under the rules, should you sign and date it.

Always show your private address in capital letters so that if this has changed from a previous year the Revenue may update their records.

· 14 ·
SOME TAX EXAMPLES

TYPICAL TAX COMPUTATION

It is very unlikely that anyone will have to fill in all the entries on a tax return, but it is important to understand how the Revenue calculates what is due for a particular period. What follows, therefore, are fairly simple examples of the tax due in a year based upon details of both earned and investment income for someone in employment.

The earnings of the taxpayer and his wife are not such that a wife's earnings election is considered appropriate as Mr A is only just into the higher-rate tax bracket. The higher-rate tax is largely due to his wife's unearned income so the wife's earnings election would convey no benefit as this is always still taxed against him.

In the example shown, there is total tax due of £5,185. If the Pay As You Earn deduction scheme has been working properly and if the unearned income had tax deducted at source, for example from bank or building society interest, then it is likely that almost all that tax will already have been received by the Revenue, so no further tax will be due from Mr A. If the difference between the amount and the calculation and the amount deducted at source on Mr A is small, for example up to £30, the Revenue may well choose not to collect it in view of the administrative costs involved.

The next calculation illustrates tax deductions at source and shows how a tax repayment can occur.

If the repayment is made on time the Revenue do not add any interest to it, but if it is delayed a repayment supplement may be due. If the tax being repaid is Schedule E tax, it is treated as being paid in the year of assessment to which the deductions relate. If the repayment is made more than twelve months after the end of that year of assessment repayment supplement will be paid from the end of the year of assessment in which the tax was paid. In effect the Revenue do not pay any interest for the first year, and then pay repayment supplement at varying rates. These approximate to $8\frac{1}{4}$ per cent at the current date.

Example 1

Facts in 1987/88

Income	Earned	Unearned
Mr A	£18,000	£1,000
Mrs A	£4,000	£7,000

Allowances/Reliefs

Mr A – Married man's allowance	£3,795	
Mrs A – Wife's earned income allowance	£2,425	
Retirement annuity paid by Mr A	£3,000	(limit 17.5% × £18,000 = £3,150)
Mortage interest paid by Mr A	£2,000	(gross)

Tax calculation

Mr A's total income	=	£30,000	(wife's income added to husband's)
Less married man's relief	£3,795		
Wife's earned income allowance	£2,425		
Retirement annuities	£3,000		
Mortage interest*	£2,000	£11,220	
		£18,780	
Tax 17,900 @ 27%	=	£4,833.00	
880 @ 40%	=	£352.00	
		£5,185.00	

If the mortgage had been paid under the MIRAS system the bill would be the same overall but the building society would have been paid £2,000 × 0.73 = £1,460 and the tax bill would be £540 greater to account for this reduction.

Example 2

	Earned Income	Tax Deducted	Unearned Income	Tax Deducted
	£	£	£	£
Mr B	20,000	4,375.35	1,000	270
Mrs B	5,000	695.25	5,000	1,350
	25,000	**5,070.60**	**6,000**	**1,620**

Reliefs/Claims Available

	£
Mr B Married man's allowance	3,795
Mrs B Wife's earned income allowance	2,425
Mr B Investment in B.E.S.* shares	5,000
Mr B Retirement annuity payment	2,000
	13,220

*Business expansion scheme

Tax Computation

Total income	£31,000
Total allowances	£13,220
Total taxable	£17,780

(Basic Rate band up to £17,900)

Tax @ 27%	£4,800.60
Tax deducted at source	£6,690.60
Repayment due:	**£1,890.00**

Comparison of UK taxes with other countries

The table below provides a comparison of tax rates around the world as a percentage of gross domestic product (GDP). The rates are intended to be only approximate because they are constantly changing:

Total tax revenue as percentage of gross domestic product at market prices

Sweden	50.5%
Denmark	49.2%
Norway	47.8%
Belgium	46.9%
France	45.6%
Netherlands	45.0%
Luxembourg	42.8%
Austria	42.5%
Ireland	39.1%
United Kingdom	38.1%
Germany	37.8%
Finland	37.3%
Greece	35.1%
Italy	34.7%
New Zealand	34.3%
Canada	33.1%
Switzerland	32.1%
Portugal	31.1%
Australia	30.3%
United States	29.2%
Spain	28.8%
Japan	28.0%
Turkey	16.1%

(*Source: Revenue statistics of OECD Countries 1965–1986*)

When Income Tax rates are considered alone it is true to say that the United Kingdom is not excessively taxed compared with other industrialised countries. In fact in many ways the various forms of tax saving investments and tax deductible items available in the UK make it a tax haven, which is why there are many foreigners who seek to become tax exiles in Britain, such as those from Sweden. This, however, only applies to Income Tax and when all other forms of taxes and duties are considered the United Kingdom's overall take of the gross national product is towards the upper end of the European league table.

It is also true to say that the United Kingdom has a relatively high starting rate of Income Tax compared with other countries and in fact is second only to Ireland. This operates against people in low-paid employment and provides a poverty trap when they try to increase their income. In addition to the United Kingdom's Income Tax starting point of 25 per cent there is, of course, the employee's national insurance contributions of some 5 to 9 per cent to consider, the threshold of which is even lower than that of Income Tax.

TAX HAVENS

In tax-haven countries such as Jersey, Guernsey and the Isle of Man the rate of tax is a standard 20 per cent. In view of the fact that they have lower tax reliefs than the United Kingdom, the effective rate of tax for those on the basic rate of 25 per cent in the UK is not now significantly different. Where the big saving comes is that the tax havens do not have the higher-rate taxes of up to 40 per cent charged in the United Kingdom, and also the Channel Islands have no Value Added Tax, though the Isle of Man does.

Other countries such as Switzerland are considered to have beneficial tax regimes. However, the benefit is confined mainly to people who have very high incomes, since rates of tax in Switzerland vary between 20 and 35 per cent. At the bottom end of the scale there is little difference between the Swiss and British rates of tax.

Most tax havens do not have Capital Gains Tax.

The 1988 changes to the United Kingdom tax system have

considerably reduced the motive for people to seek tax havens. Since setting up complicated structures often costs a considerable amount of money the United Kingdom's top rate of 40 per cent taken together with the many allowances still available means that there is no need to find a tax haven, unless you are looking for one where no tax at all is levied. It will be interesting to note what effect the latest changes have on the flourishing financial communities in the Channel Islands and the Isle of Man.

· 15 ·
PENALTIES AND RIGHTS

Comparatively few people are ever charged interest or penalised for offences concerning their tax return, but it is as well to know what the legal requirements and sanctions are.

COMPLETING THE RETURN

If no return is sent by the Revenue, that does not necessarily mean that you do not have to notify them that you are chargeable for tax. If you are taxable to income or capital gains for a particular year of assessment and have not notified the Revenue by the end of the twelve months following the end of that year, then that is an offence known as 'failure to notify chargeability' for which there is at present a maximum penalty of £100. In addition the Revenue can charge interest from the date the tax should have been paid.

The changes in the 1988 Finance Bill will bring failure to notify chargeability into line with the incorrect return offence but it is unlikely, although only experience will tell, that the penalty level will be as high as for someone who has sent in an incorrect return. The likely future penalty for a failure to notify chargeability, provided it hasn't been going on for too long, will be, it is judged, 20 per cent of the tax at stake.

If, therefore, someone has made a capital gain of £10,000 in the year to 5th April 1986 and had not let the Revenue know about it by 5th April 1987, they could be charged a £100 penalty and would have to pay the tax of £10,000 minus £5,900 at 30 per cent, which equals £1,230 as at 1st December 1986. (The £10,000 gain is assumed to be net of indexation relief). It would probably be at least six months after the due date before the Revenue could raise the assessment and therefore six month's interest at approximately 10 per cent per annum would be charged. The rate of interest is laid down by statute and there are frequent changes in line with market rates. The norm is somewhere close to the bank base rate.

FAILURE TO SEND BACK RETURNS

If the return has been sent to you by the Revenue the position is different since it can be assumed that they are aware that you are liable to Income Tax or perhaps Capital Gains Tax. The mass of tax returns are sent out early in the tax year so that the returns for 88/89 will be sent out in the second week of April 1988. In theory you have thirty days to send it back but the Revenue will accept that if the returns are back with them within, say, a five-month period, no offence has been committed and indeed the taxpayer has complied with the best practice that most accountants manage. If, however, the return is still not forthcoming, there are two avenues that the Revenue can take.

Declaring a failure

The Revenue can go to the General Commissioners or Special Commissioners of Income Tax and ask them to declare a failure that the return which was sent out on the 7th April 1988 has not been returned to them. On being presented with the evidence that the return was properly served the Commissioners will no doubt confirm a failure to make the return and can impose a fine of £50. They will then allow a period for the return to be sent in, but if it is not sent in within the requisite period it is within their powers to confirm a penalty of £10 per day for every day for which the return is still not forthcoming.

This is a comparatively long-winded procedure and there is plenty of time in which to comply with any steps that the Revenue take. It is probably in no more than one thousand cases per year throughout the country that such action would be taken by the Revenue.

Continued failure

If the failure to make the return continues after the year of assessment following that during which the return was served, there would have been a breach of the 'continued failure' rule. In such a case the Revenue can seek a penalty of £50 and 100% of the tax involved.

The normal revenue practice is to take a percentage of the penalty rather than the full amount and the percentage of tax they would charge would normally be in the 20 to 40 per cent range, depending on the circumstances of the case. It can be seen that if the amounts of the tax on the return are substantial then the amount of the penalty for continuing to hold up the return are also substantial.

It should be noted that the tax related penalty referred to can only apply if the Revenue have not raised estimated assessments on the amounts which should have been included on the return. If the Revenue have guessed that there should be income or capital gains on the return and raised assessments accordingly and used figures sufficient to cover the actual amounts due, then no tax-related penalty can arise.

INTEREST
In both of the instances referred to above there would be interest charged on the tax which should have been paid on a particular date, again at a rate of around 8 to 10 per cent.

INCORRECT RETURNS
Reference was made in an earlier chapter to the importance of the 'Declaration' at the end of the tax return. If you have submitted an incorrect return, for example leaving off £1,000 of rental income received, then the Revenue will seek a settlement requesting initially, of course, that the tax due should be paid and that interest should be paid from the date the tax was initially due, together with a tax-related penalty dependent upon the actual amount that would have been due. If it is assumed that tax of £400 is due then the tax-related penalty will be some percentage of the £400, and can of course be up to the amount of tax itself in the normal case, or indeed twice the amount of tax in the case of fraud. The normal penalty loading for such a case would be 30 to 50 per cent, so you could expect a tax penalty of, say, £160. The Revenue then seek a single cheque for the tax interest and penalty together with a declaration from the taxpayer that he has now declared everything he should have done, and has nothing further hidden from the Revenue.

The penalty for failing to inform the Revenue of an additional tax liability is to be changed from 6th April 1990. After that date the penalty will be the same as that for an incorrect return, that is up to 100 per cent of the tax involved. This substantial increase will mean that recalcitrant taxpayers will be well advised to bring their affairs up to date before 6th April 1990. The first year affected, however, is the 1988/89 tax year, since the new tax-related penalty will arise if by 6th April 1990 notification of chargeability for that tax year has not been made.

REVENUE PROSECUTIONS

The Revenue reserve the right to prosecute those who submit incorrect tax returns but would do so only in what are regarded as very serious cases. A scrutiny of the Inland Revenue Report for the period 1st January 1986 to 31st March 1987 reveals that there were only seventeen prosecutions in the period for submission of false accounts or returns of income. Indeed, the largest number of prosecutions ever revealed in the report was 39 in 1979/80 for similar offences. It is very rare for anyone to be prosecuted for an incorrect tax return but, nevertheless, it certainly can be done if someone were to complete a tax return fraudulently, under-declaring substantial sums and taking steps to hide any evidence from the Revenue.

P11D OFFENCES

Benefits provided by employers should be returned by that employer on Form P11D. The individual employee can therefore write 'per P11D' on his tax return when answering the question on benefits. However, if the employer does not submit a P11D or submits one which is incorrect, penalties can be raised upon the employer. The penalty for an incorrect P11D is £250 if the offence is neglect or wilful default, or £500 if the offence is fraud. The penalty for failing to submit the return to the Revenue is the same as that referred to above for failing to submit a tax return, that is, a maximum initial penalty of £50, and if the offence continues a penalty of £10 per day. There is no tax-related penalty for very late submission for a P11D.

It follows that if an employee does not return any benefit he receives on his individual tax return such as failing to declare that he has a company car as a benefit and if the employer also fails to mention this on the P11D then there are two offences, one committed by the employer and one by the employee. The normal Revenue practice is only to take the penalty from the employer unless the employee is a senior one who could have influenced the company returns, in which case the penalty is on both the employee and the employer. The employer is charged the maximum penalty of £250 for an incorrect return but the employee's penalty would be tax related as his is an incorrect income tax return, and this can be substantially higher than the employer's penalty.

SPECIALISED TAX RETURNS

This book has concentrated on the more usual tax returns. There are, however, a number of other returns which serve the same purpose, that is, giving the taxpayer the chance to declare to the Revenue all income received and allowing any claims for reliefs or deductions which may be due.

These are sometimes specialised because of the occupation of the taxpayer; for example, there is a special return for Lloyds underwiters, or because of the personal circumstances of the taxpayer. There is a non-resident tax return for those who have declarable income in the United Kingdom but are not actually resident. Similarly there are those who are resident in the United Kingdom who are not domiciled here and are not taxable in the UK on income or capital gains arising abroad which have not been remitted to the United Kingdom.

There are other tax returns for partnerships and trusts which again follow broadly the pattern of the normal tax return except that now the acting partner or trustee is required to fill in the return giving details of the income and captial gains of the trust or partnership for which he is acting. The individual entries on these returns largely follow those described earlier, but there are areas of difference concerning the order in which things are shown. In the trust return form 1(1NS) 1987 Boxes 5, 6, 7 referring to property in the United Kingdom are the same as Boxes 25, 26, 27 contained on the Form 11 tax return. Entries should therefore be made in exactly the same way.

REVENUE ENQUIRIES

The taxpayer's charter is reproduced as an appendix to this chapter since it illustrates the important rights that you have as a taxpayer. It should be particularly noted in the 'Fairness' paragraph that the taxpayer will have been presumed to have dealt with his tax affairs honestly unless there is reason to believe otherwise. Before the Revenue can dispute or impugn the honesty of a taxpayer they must have good reason, otherwise they are in breach of the taxpayer's charter and you can take action to ensure that fairness prevails in the manner prescribed both by the Inland Revenue and Customs and Excise department.

DATA PROTECTION ACT

The Inland Revenue are not immune from the rules of the Data Protection Act and it is possible for the taxpayer to request that the Revenue should provide him with information held upon their computer systems. The fee is currently £10 and for that the Revenue must give all the information they hold in computer format which is not exempted from disclosure.

There are apparently eight separate computer systems and a £10 fee is required for each one. All they will tell the taxpayer is the name and address under which he is entered and perhaps a few other details already known to him. It is even possible to obtain information from the Inland Revenue's investigation computer based in Liverpool so that if you have had an investigation settlement with the Revenue you can look to see how they have returned that record to Revenue Head Office. Very little is likely to be gained from interrogating the computer but for those who wish to exercise their statutory rights the opportunity is there at a relatively modest cost, although if all the files had to be researched the fee of £80 would be unlikely to be money well spent.

TAXPAYERS CHARTER JULY 1986

TAXPAYER'S CHARTER
JULY 1986

You have important rights and entitlements as a taxpayer. You are entitled to expect that:

Help and Information

- the staff of the Inland Revenue and Customs and Excise will help you in every reasonable way to obtain your rights and to understand and meet your obligations under the tax laws. So that they can do this, the Inland Revenue and Customs and Excise are entitled to expect that you will give them the full facts they need to decide how much tax you should pay.

Courtesy and Consideration

- the staff of the Inland Revenue and Customs and Excise will at all times carry out their duties courteously, considerately and promptly

Fairness

- you will have your tax liability decided impartially and be required to pay only the amount of tax properly due according to the law
- you will be treated in the same way as other taxpayers in similar circumstances
- you will be presumed to have dealt with your tax affairs honestly, unless there is reason to believe otherwise

Privacy and Confidentiality

- information about your tax affairs which is supplied to the Inland Revenue or Customs and Excise will be treated in strict confidence and used only for purposes allowed by law

Costs of Compliance

- the Inland Revenue and Customs and Excise will have regard to the compliance costs of different taxpayers (including the particular circumstances of smaller businesses). In applying their procedures, they will recognise the need to keep to the minimum necessary the costs you incur in complying with the law, subject to their duty to collect the tax that is due from you efficiently and economically.

Independent Appeal and Review

You may ask the Inland Revenue or Customs and Excise to look again at your case, if you think your tax bill is wrong or they have made a wrong decision, or they have handled your tax affairs badly. Your case can be reviewed by the head of the local office you are dealing with. If you are still not satisfied, you may take the matter up with the Inland Revenue Regional Controller or the Collector of Customs and Excise, or with their Headquarters. Beyond that, you have important rights to independent appeal.

For Inland Revenue taxes, you may appeal against your tax bill to an independent tribunal, the appeal Commissioners, and if necessary to the Courts.

For Customs and Excise taxes and duties, you may appeal against a VAT decision to the independent VAT Tribunals; or in the case of other taxes or duties directly to the Courts.

You may ask your Member of Parliament to take up your case with the office you are dealing with or with Treasury Ministers. Your Member of Parliament may also ask the independent Parliamentary Commissioner for Administration (the Ombudsman) to review your case, if you think that the Inland Revenue or Customs and Excise have handled your tax affairs improperly.

Board of Inland Revenue   **HM Customs and Excise**